Picturesque Journey

from the Northern Capital to the Ancient Capital

SAINT-PETERSBURG
MOSCOW

The State
Historical Museum

Moscow
Interbook Business
2003

The State
A.S. Pushkin Museum

SAINT-PETERSBURG

Picturesque Journey
from the Northern Capital to the Ancient Capital

MOSCOW

Interbook Business Publishers

in cooperation with

the State A.S. Pushkin Museum,
the State Historical Museum

Text and selection of illustrations by
Lydia Karnaukhova, Nonna Marchenko, the State A.S. Pushkin Museum
Marta Gurenok, Natalia Skornyakova, the State Historical Museum

Designed by
Vyacheslav Gorokhov, Aleksei Vishtalyuk

Cover by
Aleksei Vishtalyuk

Translated by
Oleg Glebov

The illustrations in the book are the property of the State A.S. Pushkin Museum,
the State Historical Museum, and the Interbook Business Publishing House

Printed by *Gorensky Tisk*, Slovenia

ISBN 5-89164-132-1

© Карнаухова Л. А., Марченко Н. А.,
  Гуренок М. К., Скорнякова Н. Н., 2003
© Иллюстрации. Государственный музей А. С. Пушкина,
  Государственный Исторический музей, 2003
© Глебов О. А., перевод на английский язык, 2003
© ЗАО «Интербук-бизнес», 2003

The picture book "Saint-Petersburg—Moscow. Picturesque Journey from the Northern Capital to the Ancient Capital" is not just another conventional coffee-table book. It is a kaleidoscopically varied presentation of engravings, water colors, an drawings created by the artists in the 18th and 19th centuries, as well as extracts from travel journals, diaries, and letters of the diplomats, authors, musicians, and famous travelers whose sincere, precise and sometimes quite unexpected comments and observations enliven the pictorial "evidence" presented in the book pages. We shall get glimpses of the Russian road scenes through the eyes of the famous Russian authors Aleksandr Radishchev and Aleksandr Pushkin, as well as such distinguished foreign visitors to Russia as Théophile Gautier, Leon de Bussier, Astolphe de Custine, Robert and Clara Schumann, Alexandre Dumas, Martha and Catherine Wilmot, Louis Philippe de Ségure and many others. Let us follow them along the highway to Moscow, see the sights and witness the magnificent festivities celebrating the coronations of the Russian monarchs. In the 18th and 19th centuries the voyage pittoresque books were very popular. In our book we shall be taking voyage not only through space but also through time traveling through the earlier history of Russia.

Visitors to Russia were always strongly attracted to its two principal cities—the magnificent European-looking Saint-Petersburg established as a modern model capital by Peter the Great and the conservative intensely traditional Moscow with deep historical roots in all aspects of life. Visitors were invariably strongly impressed with the marked contrast between the two capitals—the new one, rigorous and hard and the ancient one, cozy and colorful. One senses the contrast especially acutely when traveling through the space of seven hundred kilometers between the capitals, through the dense forests, marshes, Valdai hills, across rivers and around lakes.

We start our journey at the magnificent Saint-Petersburg with its splendid palaces, avenues, embankments, parks, and canals. It is not only architecture and views that are presented in the book. We read about the daily life of the city, the customs and mores of the populace. In their paintings artists depicted the streets full of carriages, members of the public riding and taking walks, military parades... After sightseeing in the capital of the Empire visitors embark on a long and rather tiring journey. They will pass through villages, and the ancient Russian towns of Vyshny Volochek, Torzhok, Valdai, Novgorod, and Tver where they will stay at the local inns and post stations. The towns with their ancient churches and fortifications look exquisitely charming on the scenic river banks. The provincial life is splendidly unspoiled, the living folk traditions are displayed in the costumes of the country maidens, games played by boys and girls, the Russian dances, and even in the primitive "architecture" of the Russian log cabins.

The long journey is over and the visitors finally find themselves at the ancient capital of Moscow. They are amazed to see the numerous gilded cupolas of the old churches, the opulent town mansions surrounded with lush parks, the unhurried pace of the everyday life, the charming disorder of the streets and lanes freely flowing over the legendary "seven hills" on which the first Russian capital was built.

The ceremony of coronation of the Russian tsars was traditionally performed at the Uspensky Cathedral in the Kremlin. Numerous visitors including a variety of foreign guests were attracted to Moscow by the coronation festivities. Many artists attempted to depict all the principal events of the coronation ceremonies and the festive views of the city. The best pictures were collected in the coronation albums commemorating the momentous event in the life of the Empire. The magnificent publications included engravings, water colors and lithographs. They were printed in a very small number of copies intended as mementos for the royal family members or as gifts on the most distinguished occasions. The last section of the book presenting the coronation ceremony for the Russian emperors includes some illustrations from the coronation picture albums; some of the illustrations can be seen by the general public for the first time.

Our literary and picturesque journey along the extraordinary highway originally designed by Peter the Great is ended in Moscow gaudily lit with the splendid illumination displays celebrating the coronation day.

Your expert guides on the road were the State A.S. Pushkin Museum, the State Historical Museum, and the State Literature Museum. Here is one to the road! We wish you a happy trip and memorable road impressions!

Publishing House Interbook Business

In May 1703 the Russian Tsar Peter the Great founded a new city on the banks of the River Neva to which he gave his name and attached all his hopes and aspirations. His foremost and oldest ambition was to give the Russian nation an access to a sea. Even though the Baltic Sea at the Neva estuary looked grey and unwelcoming it was opening the way to Europe. "Tsar's Peter's city" Saint-Petersburg emerged as an embodiment of the giant leap forward made by the nation spurred on by the iron will of Peter the Great. The new capital city on the grim Baltic shore was an unfamiliar "face" that the vast semi-Asiatic country turned to its Western neighbors as an emerging major player in the life of the European continent. However, Moscow, the ancient capital city, remained to be regarded as the heart of Russia, the living heritage of the centuries of national history. Two capitals represented two types of culture and these two, essentially different worlds, had to continue developing together.

The life of the road that connected the ancient capital with the Northern capital largely reflected the progress of all the attempts made by subsequent rulers to modernize Russia. The vast Russian expanses made the innovations imported from the West dissolve in the surrounding Russian reality as Russian snows inevitably melted in spring.

The first road between Saint-Petersburg and Moscow was laid through the forests and it went around bogs and marshland. The road was poorly constructed and the distances between the mail staging posts (where travelers could change horses and have a rest) were too large. In the winter time the road was frozen, traveling by sleigh was quite fast and it took three—four days to complete the trip. Peter the Great was impatient and hated the slowness and inconveniences of the travel. One of his lieutenants recalled in 1713, "I have heard that His Majesty decided to build a new road between Saint-Petersburg and Moscow that would be more than 200 miles long; it had to be not only wide but it had to be straight passing across wilderness,

forests, hills, vales, swamps and wetlands and also as smooth as possible. Moreover, it was planned to build along the road villages with mail staging posts and inns where travelers could find better amenities and travel with much greater comfort. If this project is completed it will, of course, be a great feat." Later poet Pushkin wrote facetiously,

> ...When progress and amelioration
> have pushed their frontiers further out,
> in time (to quote the calculation
> of philosophic brains, about
> five hundred years) for sure our byways
> will blossom into splendid highways:
> paved roads will traverse Russia's length
> bringing her unity and strength;
> and iron bridges will go arching
> over the waters in a sweep;
> mountains will part; below the deep,
> audacious tunnels will be marching:
> God-fearing folk will institute
> an inn at each stage of the route.

Even Peter's contemporaries saw that his project was hardly feasible. The Emperor enjoyed drawing straight lines, that was how he charted the Nevsky Prospekt in Saint-Petersburg and that was exactly as he planned the highway to Moscow—as a straight line starting at the Admiralty building in Saint-Petersburg. But the Northern nature brought about numerous obstacles to implementation of the brilliant venture. Construction engineers started their work with carefully surveying the planned route of the road. In 1710 this stage of preparations was completed but the actual road construction was started much later. In 1720 Peter the Great put out a decree on the procurement of timber "for constructing and repairing the highway to the town of Volkhov" and it was planned that the highway will be continued from Volkhov to Moscow in 1722. The highway construction was suspended after the death of the Emperor. The nobility started leaving uncomfortable Saint-Petersburg to return the customary cozy life in homely Moscow and the new capital looked almost deserted. The Imperial Court returned to Saint-Petersburg only in 1731 after enthronement of Anna Ioannovna and the need for building the highway according to Peter's plan was felt to be acute again. The through traffic over the new highway became possible only as late as 1746.

The years of the rule of Catherine the Great saw intense highway traffic between Moscow and Saint-Petersburg as court messengers rushed, government officials placidly traveled on the "business of the state", and landed gentry journeyed "for private reasons" over it. The foreign visitors and Russian travelers never missed going to the most popular sightseeing sites in Moscow and Saint-Petersburg, such as the Kremlin and the Hermitage, the Red Square and the Novodevichy Convent, and admired the Bronze Horseman and the newly erected memorial to Minin and Pozharsky. Young men dashed to Saint-Petersburg to seek out their fortunes while the retired courtiers tended to settle down in quieter Moscow. The English lady traveler Catherine Wilmot wrote in 1806, "I had an impression that I was communing with the ghosts of the Court of Catherine the Great in Moscow which looked like the Imperial Elysium."

The life in the ancient capital demonstrated some signs of a genuine revival only during the coronation festivities. The old tradition was to perform the ritual at the Uspensky Cathedral in the Kremlin. The coronation pronouncement was sent out to all corners of the country and heralds read it out ("shouting at the top of their voices") at the Ivanovskaya Square in the Kremlin. The Emperor or the Empress arrived from Saint-Petersburg at an early date and stopped at the Petrovsky Travel Palace just outside Moscow. The Imperial train entered Moscow proper with appropriately ceremonial fanfare precisely on the coronation day.

It was a great day for the spectators who liked to reminisce about it. Artists sketched the views before executing paintings and engravings intended for a special coronation picture book to be published later. The festivities continued for several days. Then the Court returned to Saint-Petersburg where official receptions were continued for foreign representatives and awards were given out while Moscow gradually calmed down returning to its usual serene way of life.

The highway between Saint-Petersburg and Moscow had to be well prepared to ensure comfortable travel for the Imperial train carrying the Emperor and his retinue including numerous courtiers. The road surface was repaired and for some time carriages of the commoners were not allowed to travel by it to preserve the even surface freshly sprinkled with sand. But the excellent road surface was usually ruined soon after the Imperial train had passed. Aleksandr Radishchev noted that in his "Journey from Saint-Petersburg to Moscow" in 1790: "When I started from Saint-Petersburg I assumed that the road quality was very good. Everybody who had traveled along the road soon after the Emperor said that it was excellent. Indeed, it was excellent but only for a short time. The dirt on the road made its surface smooth when it was dry but when it rained it made the road non-passable..."

Innumerable potholes, ruts, and ditches made the carriages jolt continuously causing a lot of suffering for the travelers. Contemporaries told a story about Catherine the Great who wished to make an impression on the Austrian Emperor Joseph by taking him at a great speed from Saint-Petersburg to Moscow. A carriage driver was found who said he could make the trip in 36 hours. When he was taken to meet the Empress he said, "Your Majesty, I can indeed take the German king from Saint-Petersburg to Moscow in 36 hours but I cannot promise that his soul will stay within his body."

The travelers who took the road from Saint-Petersburg to Moscow or back had a rather limited range of impressions. The road brought them to only two cities—Tver and Veliky Novgorod. They were in a hurry to reach their destination, did not pay much attention to the sights noting only that they were "quite boringly identical". Some entertainment, however, was available along the route: at the town of Valdai famous bagel-type cakes were baked, at the town of Torzhok an inn served excellent chicken-meat balls and one could buy in the local market distinctive belts and other locally made leather goods. Foreign travelers were fascinated with the Russian folk festivals. They were duly impressed with the forbidding vast expanses of Russia that shaped the character of the people inhabiting them. Foreigners never tired of complaining about various hardships of their travel in Russia. Their diaries, road journals, and reminiscences are full of "road grumbles"...

What evil spirit took me to this road,
    the frozen ocean of woe?
What cruel tempest hurled my carriage
    in the waves of snow,
The waves that rock and shake it,
    never letting go.
The carriage drops and jumps
    and downslides again,
Is thrown back and forth but is not moving on.

Travel, indeed, was not easy in those days! Travelers could use their own horses and carriages and then they had to stay at road inns for a day or two to give horses a rest. The other option was to travel in one's own carriage by "stages" changing horses at each mail stage post. Martha Wilmot wrote in her diary on March 26, 1808, "What a misery traveling in Russia is even by the main highway between Saint-Petersburg and Moscow. It is impossible to procure a change of mail horses for any payment. It is simpler for General Laptev who immediately attacks the stage-post keeper with his fists or a cane if he is detained

for at least five minutes. The effect is immediate and the keepers start trying to make him happy. What can be done by more peacefully-minded travelers, though? If you give the keeper some money he immediately gets drunk and nothing can be gained as he becomes completely incapacitated." There were often not enough horses at a stage post and travelers had to wait for a change of horses to return from the next stage and to give them time to rest. At any moment a high official, an important member of the aristocracy, or a government messenger could commandeer the fresh change of horses and the ordinary traveler was left with no choice but more waiting.

As early as 1820 the main Russian highway saw the first public carriages modeled on the European stagecoaches. The Saint-Petersburg newspaper "Severnaya Pchela" wrote on September 2, 1830, "The stagecoach company which operated for ten years under a license will continue functioning after expiration of the license. The successful operation of the first Russian company of that type is the beneficial product of the efforts of the benevolent government intent on working for the public good. The mail authority which was charged with overseeing the enterprise did everything in their power to promote the new activity. The grateful founders of the company will spare no effort to improve further the efficiency of the endeavor."

The stagecoaches for long journeys accommodated from four to six persons on a single level. Before the introduction of public stagecoaches travelers preferred to take relatives or servants into their carriages or sometimes placed advertisements in newspapers about vacant carriage seats available (but always made travel arrangements with strangers well before the journey). In the first years since the introduction of the public stagecoaches people felt quite self-conscious when having to take seats side by side with complete strangers. Aleksandr Pushkin complained in a letter to his wife, "...just imagine who were my fellow-travelers, with whom I spent five days and nights side by side. You'd be cross with me! It was five German actresses in short yellow coats and black veils. How do you like it? Believe me, my dear, I never made advances to them, it was them who flirted with me hoping that I shall buy more tickets. But I declined indicating that I did not know German."

It was assumed that traveling by a stagecoach was safer. Unfortunately, it was not always the case. Pushkin's mother, Nadezhda, wrote to her daughter on May 8, 1833, "I embarked on the journey feeling entirely confident that the stagecoach could not break down and hoping that I should travel through day and night and sleep quietly. But I had a terrible scare, just as I started dozing I sensed that the carriage was close to overturning and spilling us out. We were fortunate, though, and easily came out through the door. It was not raining but a very strong wind was blowing, one had to clutch the hat and the coat while running for eight miles. Father was desperate, I kept on thinking how to find some help and asked a passing peasant woman about any manor houses along the road. She mentioned Lady Khrapovitskaya who lived 5 miles from Tver and I immediately sent a servant on horseback to beg her for assistance. She invited us for tea..." Recollections of such road adventures were quite common. In their letters the Russian travelers only rarely described the sights they encountered along the road but foreign visitors typically noted much. For a Russian the highway leading from the old capital to the new one was merely a road he was obliged to take. Taking that road was not an easy accomplishment even though Pushkin praised the smoothness of the newly surfaced highway in his "Journey from Moscow to Petersburg".

In 1839 Marquis de Custine gave the following warning: "A traveler in Russia is faced with a hazard which one can hardly expect, namely, that his head can be broken by the top of his carriage. The risk is great, indeed, and

the hazard is quite feasible. The carriage is thrown up and down by the road potholes, by the logs with which bridges are constructed, or by the numerous tree stumps dotting the road surface and a voyager is faced with the sad alternative of being thrown out from the carriage if the top is down or to shatter his skull if the top is up. That is why in Russia one should use a carriage whose top is removed as far from the seat as possible." Marquis de Custine went on telling his European readers about the Russian roads laid through the marshes in the age-tried manner as pavements made of logs simply placed across the road (when the logs sank into the marsh new logs were put on top of them). A carriage passed over such log road surface as a hand along a keyboard and no spring suspension could protect a traveler from incessant heavy bumping.

The first railroads were built in Europe in the early 19th century. The first railroad in Russia was built between the towns of Pavlovsk and Tsarskoe Selo near Saint-Petersburg where major Imperial Court palaces were located. Initial trains of carriages had been driven by horses but soon steam engines were introduced. The first steam train made a trip on September 27, 1836. An official ceremony marking the opening of the Tsarskoe Selo railroad was held a year later, on October 30, 1837. The onlookers and the passengers were delighted with the amazing sights. The "Severnaya Pchela" newspaper published a report saying that "the passengers were accommodated in the comfortable and spacious carriages, wagons, and coaches according to their wishes and the prices of the tickets they acquired at the booking office; just as they took their seats the long train of twelve huge carriages majestically started moving as the bell rang out. Indeed, it was something looking like sorcery! Do you hear the ferocious deafening roar of the fiery stallion emitting dense clouds of smoke? One can imagine nothing more magnificent than this force, overwhelming yet manageable, which flies faster than the wind. A joyful scream is emitted by the arrogant and mighty steam engine at the first stepson it calms down and runs steadily on... The passengers sitting in the carriages do not feel any motion—everything around them flies with them, the wind beats its wings over their faces cooling down the hot brows, the heart beats slowly and one feels as if sliding, rather than running, along the railroad and arrives when feeling just getting ready to leave."

The newspaper "Sankt-Peterburgskie Vedomosti" wrote on February 13, 1837, that unaccustomed public was so endangered by approaching the engines "that it was only the exceptional care that could prevent accidents and the steam engines could not be run at full speed permitted by the full steam power".

As early as January 21, 1836 poet Petr Vyazemsky wrote to his friend Aleksandr Turgenev about an extraordinary piece of news concerning the plans on building the railroad between Pavlovsk and Tsarskoe Selo. He continued, "...there are even proposals for building a railroad between Saint-Petersburg and Moscow but there is an opposition to them. As for me, I believe that there is yet much to be done in Russia before building railroads." He added, however, "Of course, it was the heavy hand of Peter's which prodded us into action, it took us days to grow into a shape that took other nations years, we moved in leaps rather than in steady steps, that seems to be our destiny."

Indeed, immediately after the Tsarskoe Selo railroad had been built the Russian government started discussing plans for the Saint-Petersburg—Moscow railroad. Two options were considered—building the railroad along the existing highway through Novgorod Veliky or laying a straight route between two capitals. The Emperor Nikolai I commanded building the railroad in a straight line saying that there "was not a single good reason for passing the railroad through Novgorod which should never lose the advantages it enjoys at present". There is a well-known story about Nikolai I drawing a straight line between

Saint-Petersburg and Moscow on the map but making a small curve around his finger holding the ruler. The construction engineers were afraid to question the plans drawn by the royal hand and build the railroad exactly reproducing on the ground what they saw drawn on paper. This story is hardly true. The route of the future railroad was carefully investigated and it was Peter the Great himself who had drawn the route of the planned highway between two capitals in a straight line.

The railroad construction was proceeding in two sections simultaneously—between Saint-Petersburg and the town of Chudovo and between the town of Vyshny Volochek and the city of Tver. There were scheduled trains running between Saint-Petersburg and the suburban town of Kolpino as early as 1846. According to the "Severnaya Pchela" newspaper a daily passenger train left Saint-Petersburg at 11 a.m. and a freight train left at 8 a.m. In 1849 the railroad segments between Saint-Petersburg and the town of Chudovo and between the town of Vyshny Volochek and the city of Tver were opened for traffic. The entire railroad was completed and services were officially launched on November 1, 1851. Large bridges were built across the rivers Volkhov, Msta, Tvertsa, and Volga. The railroad crossed hills, woods, and marshes, deep trenches had to be dug out while some sections had to be raised high to make the road flat and from the station Kryukovo down to Moscow the railroad was passing at a constant slope.

A passenger train took 48 hours to cover the distance between Saint-Petersburg and Moscow in summer or winter. That seemed to be a fantastic speed. The contemporaries felt as if they were flying, rather than riding the train. Poet Petr Vyazemsky wrote,

It flies like lightning, fast and fey,
It leaves no trace like air wave,
The hills and cities pass as ghosts,
As shades of towns flying by,
And distant sights seem to be lost...
The rush, the haste cause thoughts to fade,
Your mind is blurred, your soul is dazed,
You dash ahead with gasping breath...

The opening of the railroad link between two capitals was a high point of the long years of the reign of Nikolai I. In honor of the occasion the Emperor was presented with an album containing ten views of the railroad showing stations, locomotives, bridges and trains (now it is the property of the Russian State Library in Moscow). The water colors for the album were executed by the architect and artist Avgust Petzold (1823/24—1891) who was elected to the Academy of Arts after that.

Russia was entering into a new era of its history. An essentially new mentality was replacing the old Russian way of thinking as life in all its aspects was increasingly gaining a novel much faster pace. The old capital and the new capital strove to preserve their original character while rushing headlong into the turbulent 20th century towards their destiny which was to be equally challenging for both of them.

Saint-Petersburg

People who have visited all European capitals say that neither of them can be compared to Saint-Petersburg… One cannot be but amazed and impressed when seeing the vast streets, squares, embankments, wide canals leading to the Neva River, and numerous palaces and houses that sprang to life as if by magic…

François Ancelot

*I love you, city willed by Peter,
I love your graceful somber views,
The stately flow of Neva's waters
Amid the granite buttressed banks...*

           Aleksandr Pushkin

The founding of Saint-Petersburg signifies the mighty power of the Russian will, the one which meets no unsurmountable obstacles.

           Louise Germaine de Staël

We see Falconet's bronze before us, that wondrous steed, vigorous, fierce, handsome and so boldly erected that a foreigner impressed with the daring concept said to me, indicating the sculpture, "It dashes on as Russia does!"

           Konstantin Batyushkov

The monument commemorating Peter I is the only one of its kind in the world in beauty and magnificence as it wonderfully blends audacity and excellence so evocative of the glory of the Great Monarch whom it depicts and the enterprising Genius of the lady who erected it.
The guilt inscriptions on pedestal of the monument carry a brief but powerful message in Latin on one side and in Russian on the other side:
To Peter the First
Catherine the Second
Year 1782.

           Pavel Svinyin

..We stayed at the new Winter Palace which was rebuilt after the fire in the almost original form in an incredibly short time... We went through the Winter Palace which is so large that one can easily lose one's way in it...

Friedrich Hagern

The proud palace boasts of its glory,
The splendid columns line the façade marble;
The playful putti figures are laughing from the wall,
Through windows it's luxury and never-ending ball,
Lush flowers, rich dresses flash through mirrored hall...
　　　　Semen Nadson

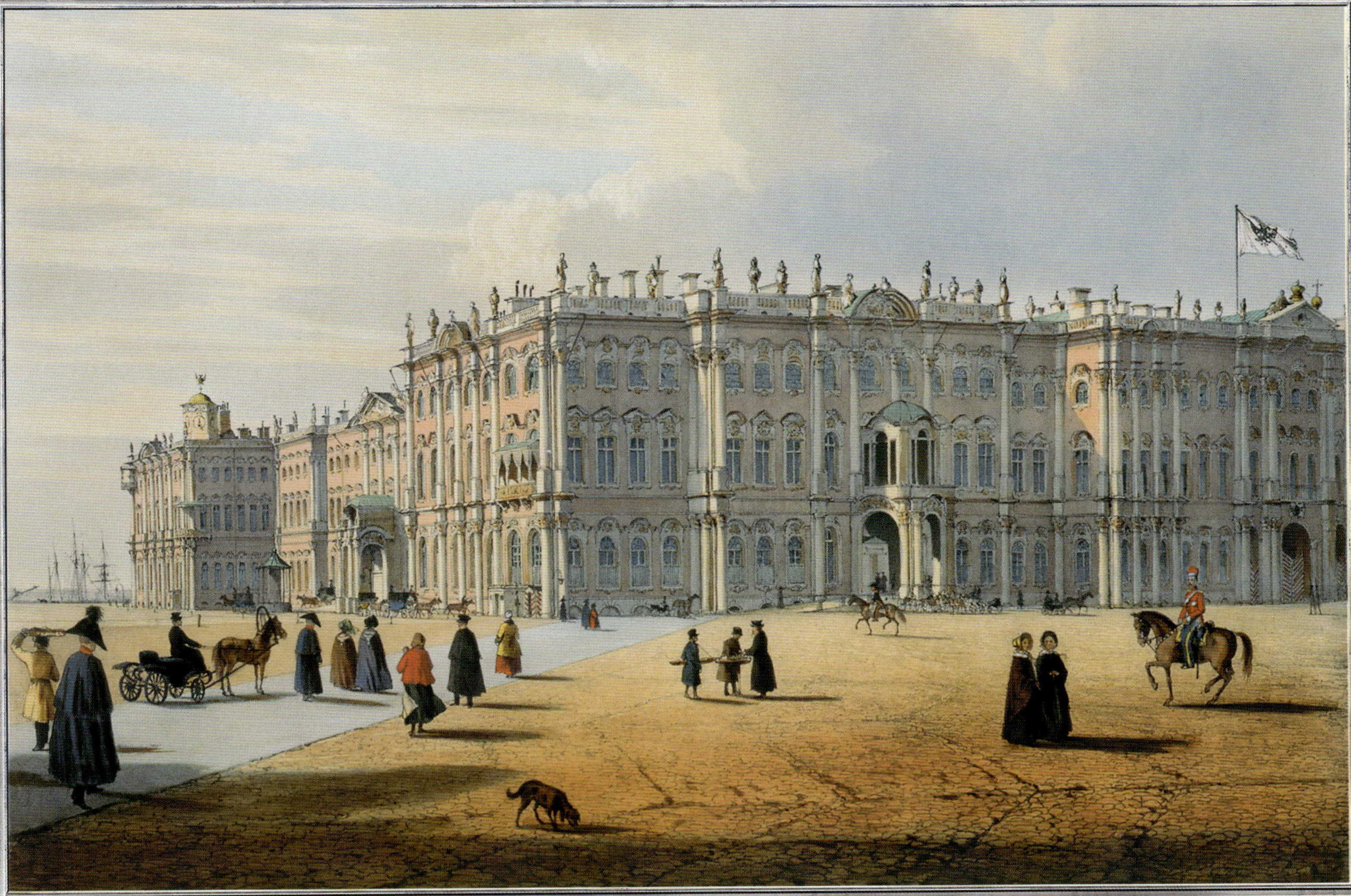

...A magnificent throne was installed at the Georgievskaya Hall in 1794. Six marble steps went up to the throne, lined with side walls bearing arches and ornaments, the back wall had a rich marble epistyle; two large marble vases and the statues symbolizing "Faith" and "Law" stood on both sides...The architect Starov designed the throne.

Mikhail Pylyaev

Finally I reached the palace chapel, though it took me some effort...
The palace chapel is rather small...
The chancel is surrounded with a baluster railing. The chancel is a fairly low square altar. The space immediately before the chancel allocated to the members of the Emperor's family was still free.

Astolphe de Custine

There are the portraits on the palace wall…
The Tsar has ordered artists to paint all
Commanding generals of glorious Russian army
That crushed invading hordes and saved us from infamy,
That marched to vanquish foes in grandeur unsurpassed.

Aleksandr Pushkin

8

It is impossible not to be astonished by the
magnificence and power of the New Rome!

"Severny Vestnik", 1804

*The giant palaces are standing noble guard
Along the proud river in a row...*
  Petr Yakubovich

⑨

...A visitor cannot help being surprised and impressed by the city whose magnificent regularity dazes and amazes him and at the same time whose uniformity makes him weary. Indeed, there are cities in the world that are larger than Saint-Petersburg but neither of them seems to be larger; here is no single curved line here, no tricky turn than can make you misjudge the distance.

  François Ancelot

The first object is the brilliantly and austerely planned building of the Winter Palace; you can see its façade opposite the Admiralty. Then you come to see the great semi-circle of the General Staff rimming the Palace Square distinguished by its bold archway, the Corinthian columns, trophies, majestic frieze and triumphal chariot crowning its noble pinnacle.

Aleksandr Bashutsky

O proud Neva, flow easily
Around monuments of kings,
The shady isles are sleeping dreamily
As church bell steadily rings.

              Mikhail Muravyev

12

Just look how harmonious the city is! how all its elements blend into a single entity! how beautiful the buildings are, how tasteful everything is and how varied are the sights of water blending with architecture.

              Konstantin Batyushkov

...The Tavrichesky Palace with a level rotunda is surrounded with a dense and wide park on the other bank of the river... The Potemkin's dream embodied in stone does not seem particularly imposing at a close range but it looks strikingly impressive at a large distance when one sees its general outline and not the minor details.

              Alexandre Dumas

Neva, its embankments and bridges make up the genuine glory of Saint-Petersburg. The river is so wide that everything seems tiny beside it. Neva seems to be a vessel filled with water to the brim and the water seems ready to spill over at any moment.

Astolphe de Custine

The river is lined with an embankment of pink granite, it looks majestic when calm and frightening when stirred, boats carrying colored flags of all nations are swaying on its azure waves almost all year long...The Neva river embodies the beauty of Saint-Petersburg, its glory, its treasures, and its horror.

Sophie Choiseul-Gouffier

The river Neva is magnificent... It is thanks to the majestic river that Saint-Petersburg benefits from such impressive sights that can be found only in very few capital cities.

Alexandre Dumas

Each morning a flag is raised on the 7-fathom-high masthead on the Saint-Catherine bulwark, the flag is lowered down at sunset and serves as a signal to ships… Before the reign of Pavel I the raising of the flag was marked by firing a cannon during the entire season when Neva was free of ice… On holidays a large yellow flag was raised which carried the Russian heraldic sign of the eagle whose claws and wings represented four Russian seas—White, Black, Caspian and Baltic; a cannon was fired from the bulwark to mark the dawn, the midday, and the sunset.

Pavel Svinyin

*I saw Neva, I saw the fortress and the bridge,
Academy of Arts, Saint Isaacs, and Exchange,
The staff of dreams, the sense of beauty which
The city gives you at whatever range...*

Lev Mey

The people who have visited all European capitals claim that none of them can be compared to Saint-Petersburg. I must admit, my friend, that one cannot but be astonished and overwhelmed when one sees the vast avenues too long for a glance to cover them, squares, embankments, wide canals joining the Neva River, numerous palaces and edifices erected, as if by a magic force, on the swampy land where a hundred years ago there had been only muddy bogs that had seemed to be no fit place for a human being.

François Ancelot

20

21

The Exchange building in Bordeaux that was regarded as the most magnificent one in Europe must surrender its place as the largest and most beautiful building to the new Saint-Petersburg Exchange which is not only architecturally great but has the most pleasant and advantageous location. It has been built on a promontory formed by the Neva River on one side and by its main branch, known as the Small Nevka, on the other side.
A large semi-circular space before the front façade facing the Neva River is intended for unloading and storing goods. The embankment is built with granite slabs which slope towards the water level at two sites... Two impressive columns have been erected at the sides of the square; they carry decorations in the shape of ship's prows and several impressive sculptures the most remarkable of which is the huge statue of Neptune. Steep staircases inside the columns allow one to climb up to their tops which are rather wide platforms surrounded with iron railings. If the weather is clear one can enjoy the most beautiful views looking from the columns. The huge stone edifices seem to be rising straight from the waters surrounding the capital.

Pavel Svinyin

*Look at the trooper, neat and smart,
Always ready and polite,
He is worldly, he is bright,
He's from Europe all right...*

Fedor Glinka

... We were woken by the noise made by the horses and troops under our windows. They were getting ready for the scheduled garrison parade. The parade started at about 10 in the morning. The even rows of soldiers marching in their brand-new uniforms presented a brilliant sight, indeed. The Emperor was riding along the ranks. He looked so much like his likenesses that are sold in all shops that it was simply impossible not to recognize him.

Martha Wilmot

*A solid stone wall topped by impressive spire
Stands face to face with gaudy city views,
As if all set to bring regretful news
It looks at them across the wide Neva.*

          Sergei Andreevsky

(24)

The Peter-and-Paul Fortress accommodates the Peter-and-Paul Cathedral where there are the burial vaults of the members of the Imperial family. The tombstones over the vaults are shaped as coffins draped with rich fabrics and standing in the church...
The fortress also houses the first Russian ship built by Peter the Great, at least he did some handwork over it. The ship bears the seed of the Russian naval might.

          Friedrich Hagern

(25)

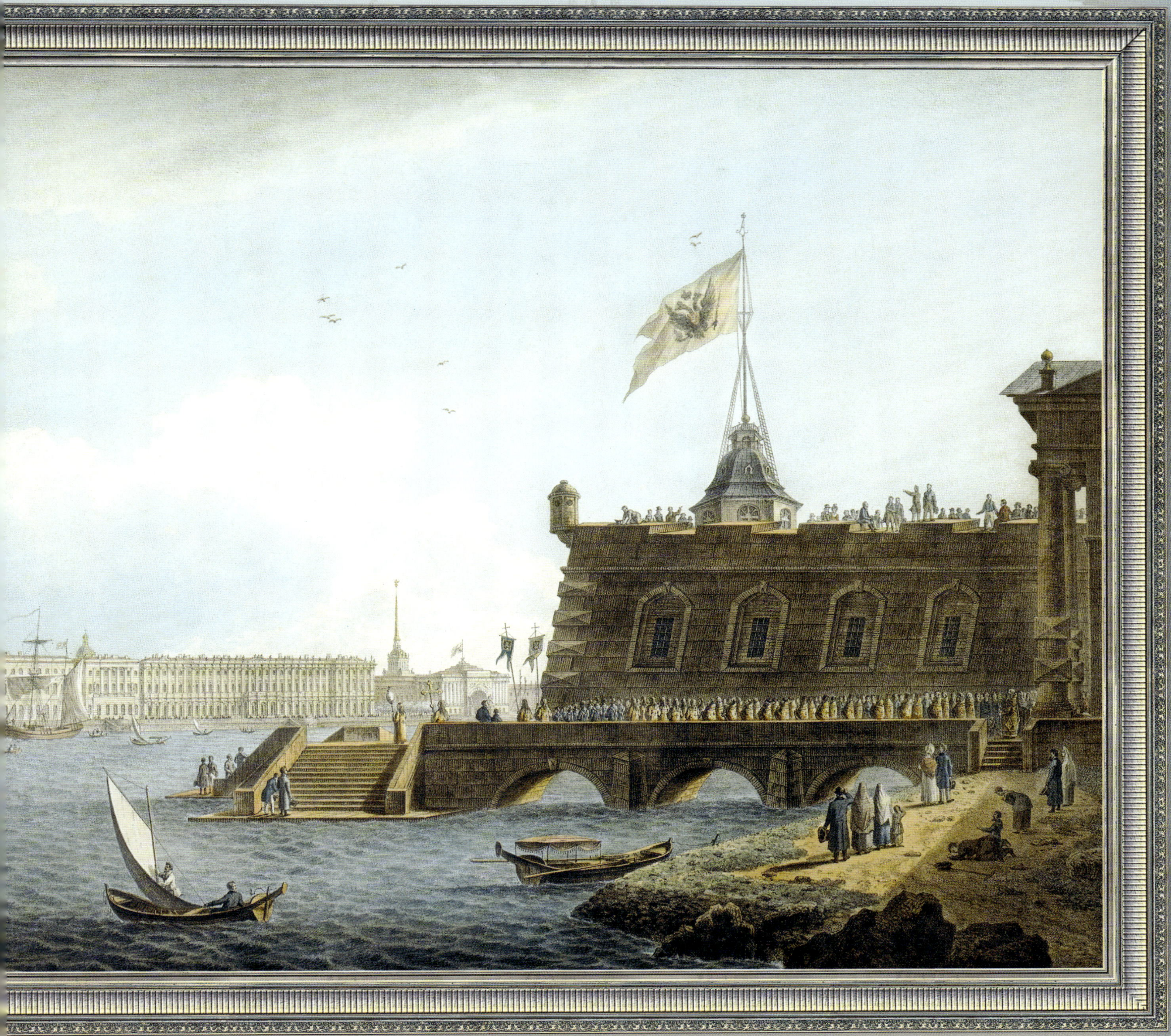

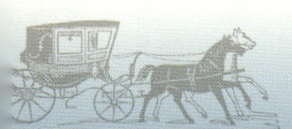

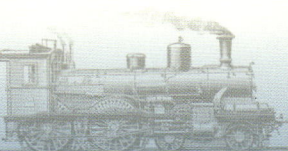

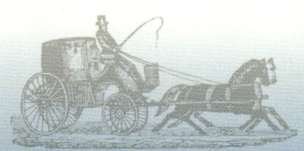

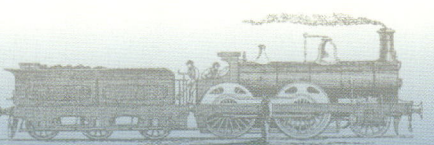

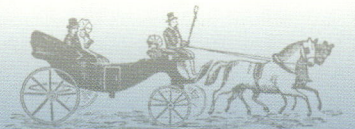

I have never seen anything more splendid than the Neva—a full clear-water river that is typically calm. Right now (I can see it in my window) there are 10—12 nice-looking attractively decorated rowing boats on the water half of which are shaded by tents with gilt fringes. The movements of the rowing oarsmen are strikingly harmonious, after each pull of the oars they pause impressively while they keep singing and the melodies of their tunes are said to be unlike all other songs of the Russian people...

I often visit the Hermitage Palace, ride in a boat on the magnificent Neva River, visit some parks, and the Saint Catherine Institute. Nothing can be compared to Saint-Petersburg in summer—it is splendid throughout day and night while the night here can hardly be called that... In the darkest night hours one has enough light to read and work. The house (of the d'Ogie family) stands on a bank of the great Neva River, in my opinion its beauty is on par with the best Venetian sights. As in Venice, we are riding along the river on small boats with tents many of which are moored along the river bank.

Martha Wilmot

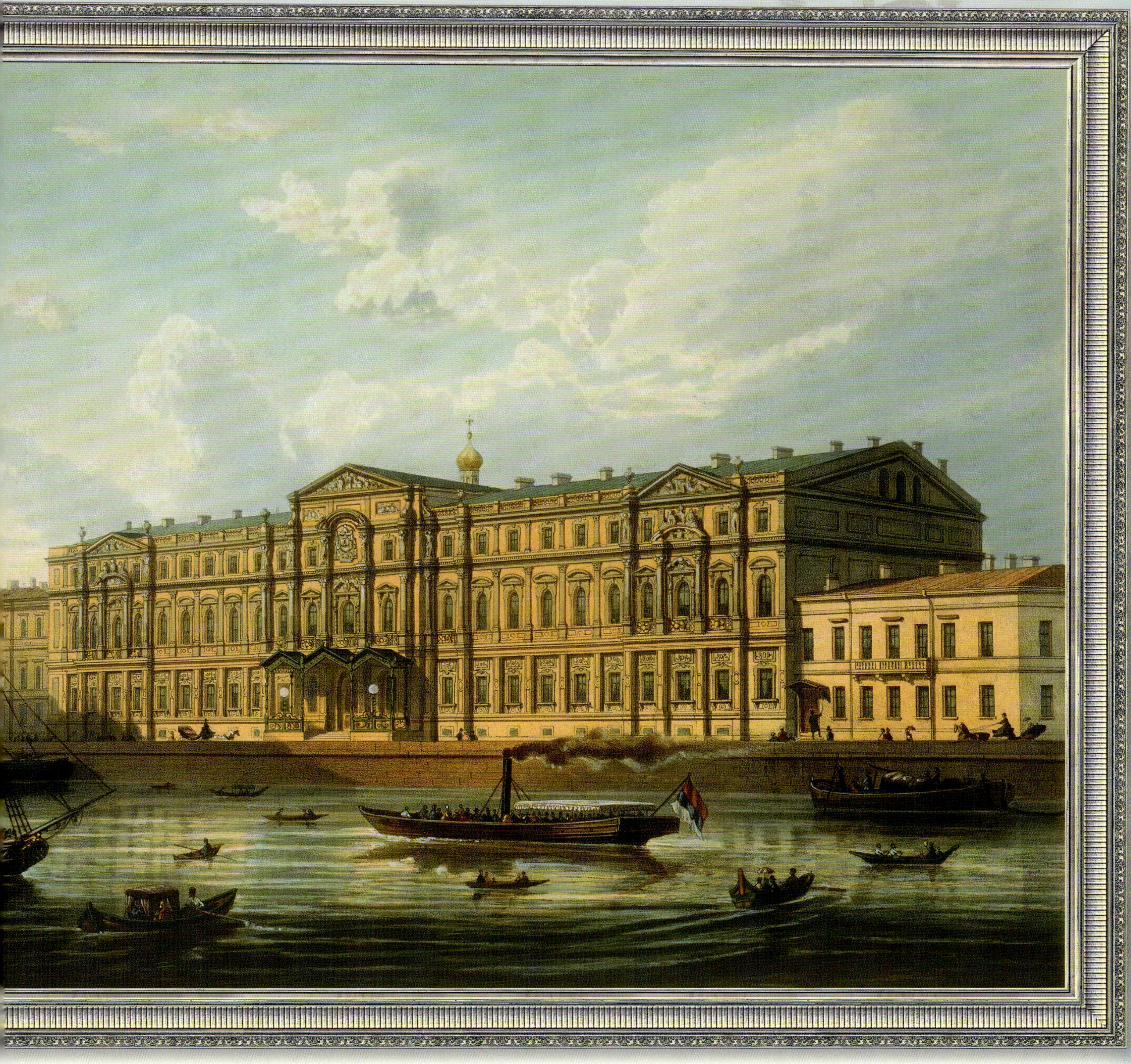

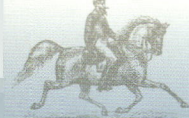

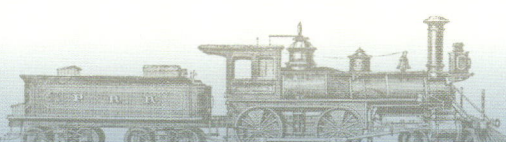

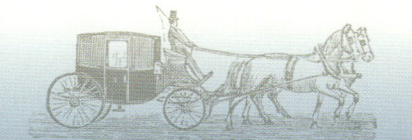

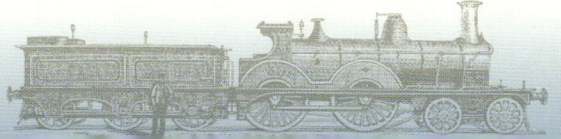

The city has been opulently built,
Its church spires have been gilt,
Its towers are reaching to the heaven,
Rich are its streets and theaters, and dwellings.

        Nikolai Nekrasov

...It is the archway between the Hermitage and the Theater. We have chosen this sight because it is richly picturesque as the arch is cleverly built and very beautiful... One is invariably astounded to see at once a boat passing under a granite bridge, the carriages on the bridge and under the arch, and the visitors crowding the gallery.

        Pavel Svinyin

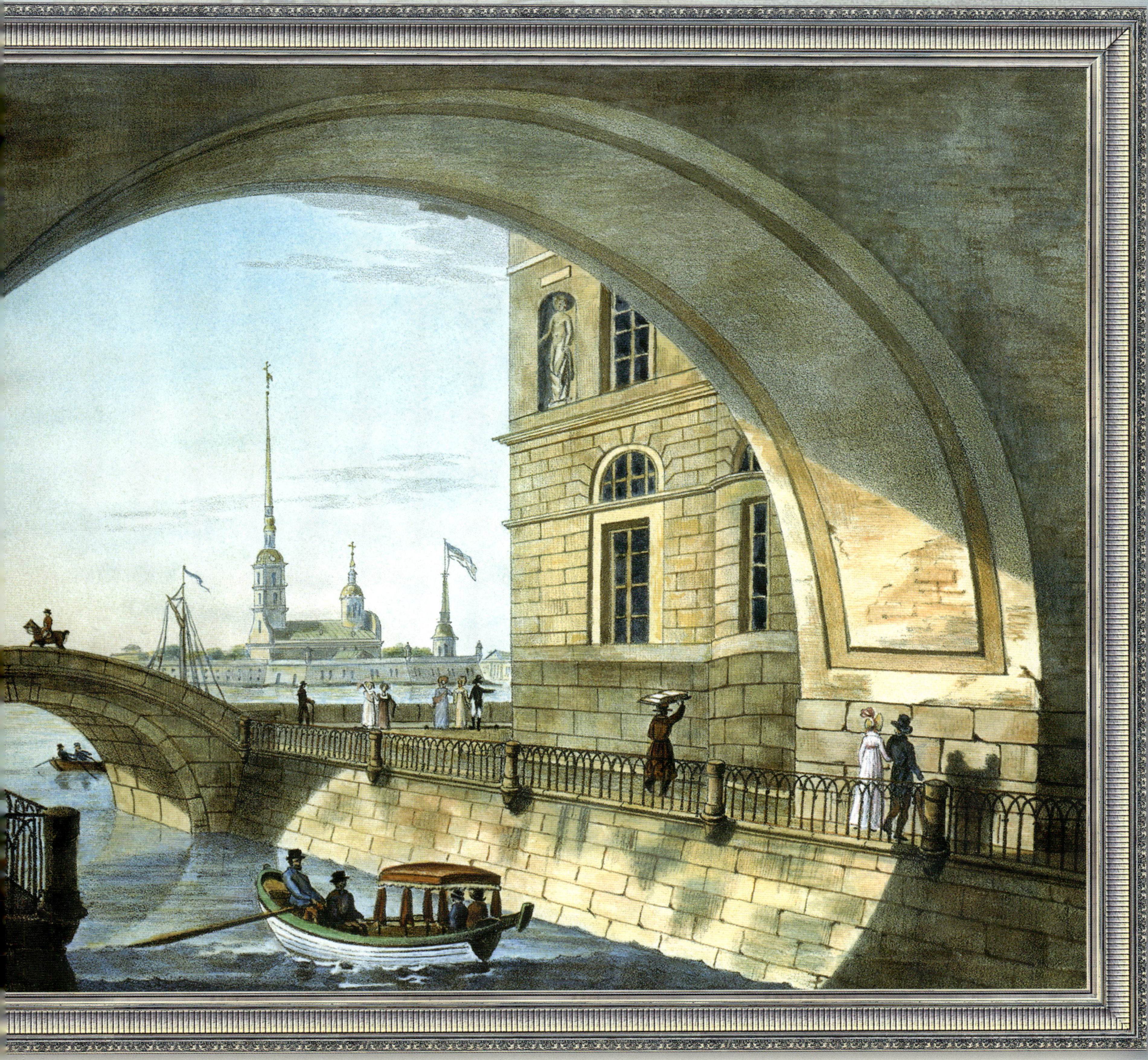

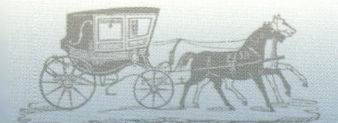

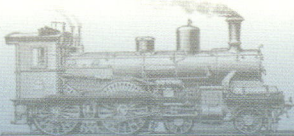

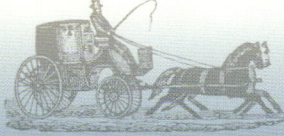

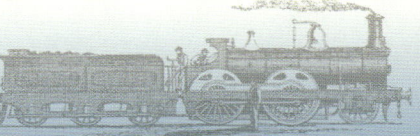

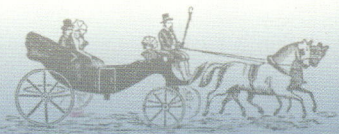

30

42

*The palaces along the river banks
Seem brooding shades of former glories...*
   Mikhail Lermontov

The embankments are the most wonderful attractions of Saint-Petersburg, there is nothing like them in the whole world—so charming, so spacious and so extensive they are.

Vladimir Mikhnevich

...The carriage turned into the Angliiskaya Embankment lined with the façades and porticos of the palaces or no less gorgeous detached town houses painted in bright colors with balconies and loggia overhanging over the pavement... When I was passing by I looked into the low windows and admired the banana trees and tropical plants growing in the warm living rooms resembling hothouses.

Théophile Gautier

In the former foggy marshes,
Drenched eternally with dew
There's a fountain that gushes
In the blooming garden new.

Sergei Soloviev

But the most remarkable decoration of the garden was its railing fence stretching along the Neva bank. A high wrought-iron grille is mounted on a granite base between granite columns topped with vases...
At that time the grill was gilded with real gold because gilding was executed at the time of Catherine the Great... The guilt grille was shining in the sun and was famous for its splendor. Many foreign visitors came specially to see it. There is a story that a rich Englishman, a Lord, left London on board his own yacht, arrived into the Neva, cast his anchor opposite the Summer Garden, looked with admiration at the magnificent railing without leaving his yacht and immediately left for Britain saying only, "It is very good!"

Pavel Sokolov

One of the advantages of the garden is that when you visit it you are always breathing clean country air while still at the heart of the capital city... You have before your eyes beauties of the countryside nature and the amazing works of the human genius. Just make a step out of the garden gate and you emerge into the Palace Embankment. There you are facing the majestic Neva with merchant ships on it, across the quiet azure river waters you see the forbidding Peter-and-Paul Fortress, a bit further you see the new Exchange with columns resembling an ancient temple and the grand buildings around it...

Pavel Svinyin

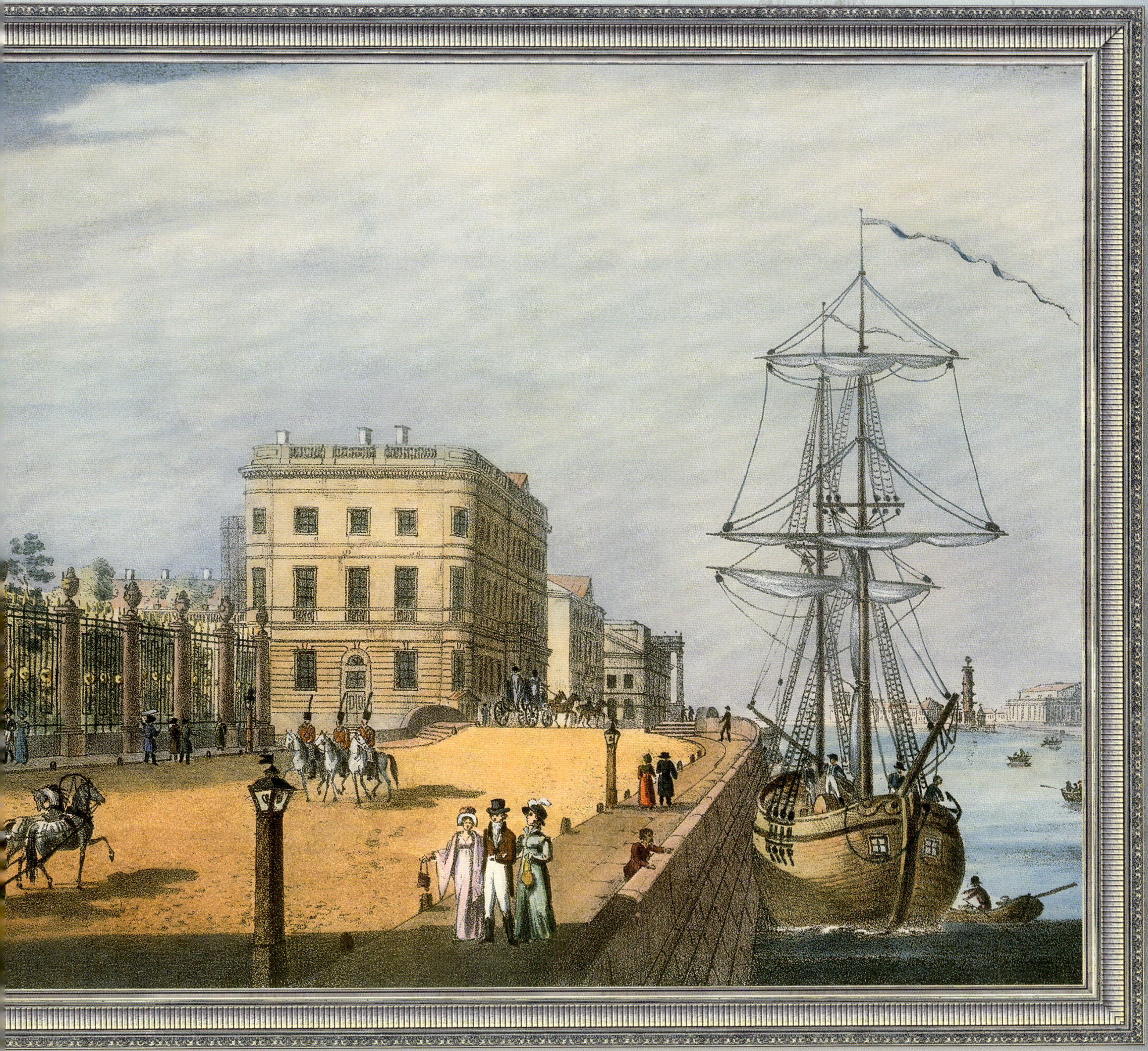

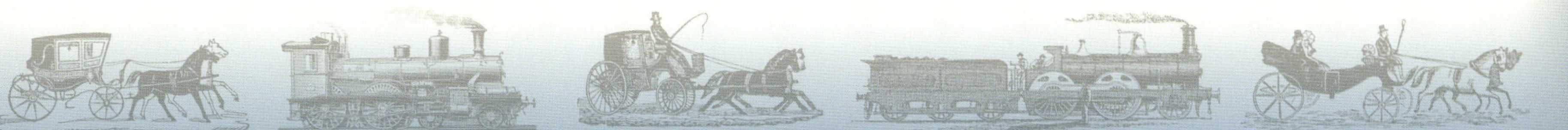

A few days ago I experienced for the first time a sleigh ride down an ice slope about which you may have read in a book on the history of amusements in Saint-Petersburg. It is extremely entertaining. We went at least 80 feet up by a ladder and at the top we saw a lovely booth decorated with green pine branches from which an ice slope with trees on both sides went down to the ground. The slope was sprinkled with water which immediately froze to a perfectly smooth ice... A man on skates standing at the back of a high sleigh pushes it and slides down together with it while directing its slide. You slide down in a flash and cannot stop until the slope ends. I felt as if I was flying through the air as a bird.

Martha Wilmot

I love your frost and snow,
I love your winters harsh,
Along the wide Neva in sleigh I go
And pretty maidens gently flush.

Aleksandr Pushkin

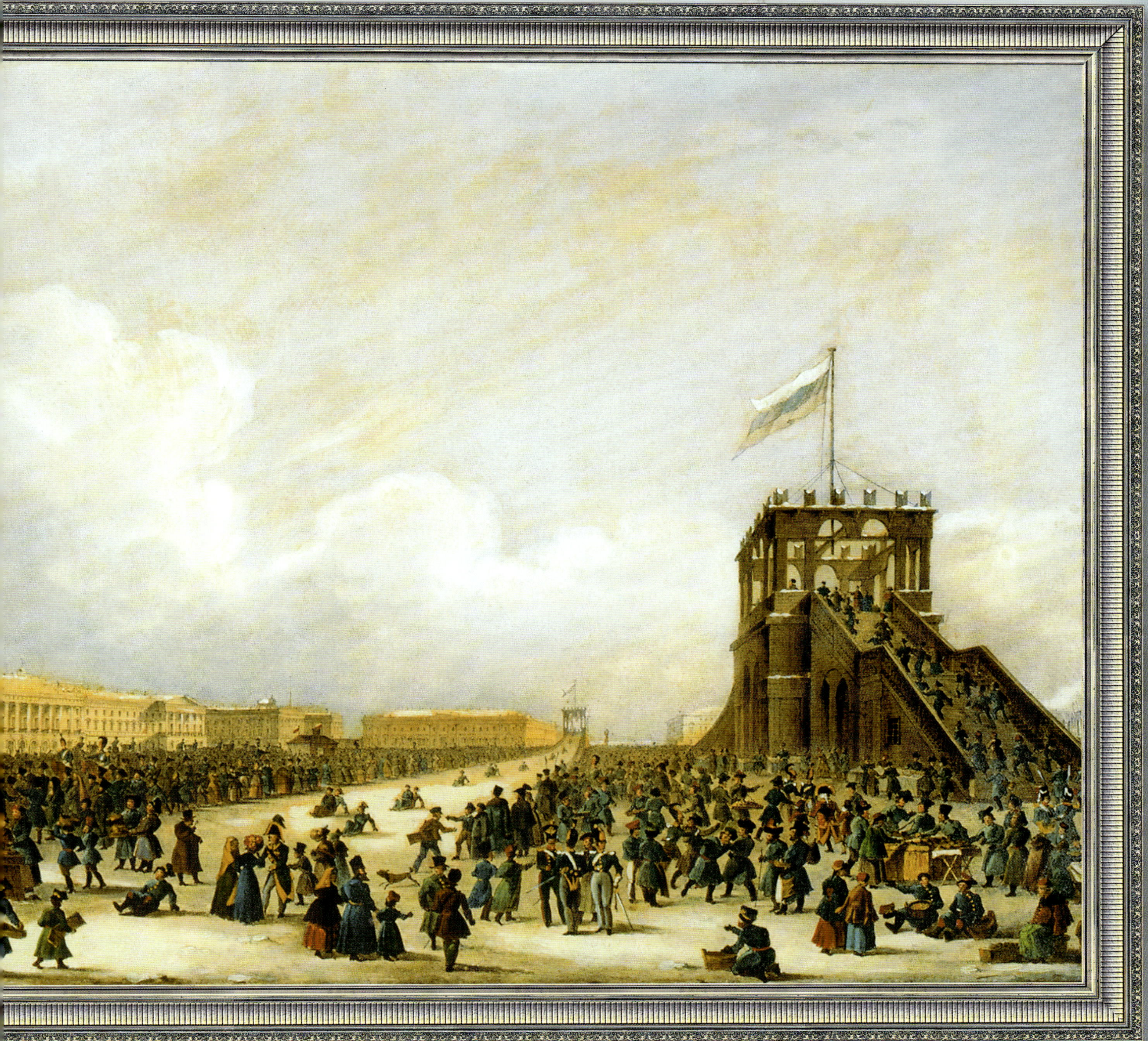

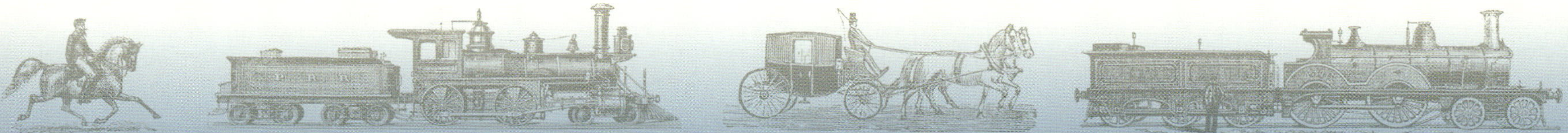

36

*In the scarlet sky the gems are falling
Deep into the waters light
That deep in the canals are flowing
Guarded by the railings closed tight.*

Vladimir Knyazhnin

48

Numerous canals crisscross the city that is built on many islands like a Northern Venice. Three canals intersect the Nevsky Prospekt that passes above them: the Moika canal, the Ekaterininsky Canal, and then the Ligovka Canal and Fontanchik.

Théophile Gautier

39

*You will in the city readily find
Museums of antiques, all "vestiges of learning",
All to improve your mind…*
  Nikolai Nekrasov

40

I kept on admiring the edifice that bears witness to the intelligence of Catherine, the benefactor of sciences and arts. At each step here an erudite patriot should call blessings in the memory of the Monarch whom the grateful posterity gave the title of Great and Wise in honor of her constructive deeds, rather than her conquests. How many worthy men were given to the society through the service of the Academy of Arts! Very few institutions in Russia produced so many benefits.

  Konstantin Batyushkov

41

52

I was also impressed with the magnificent and regular beauty of Saint-Petersburg: the wide endless avenues are lined with trees and the pavements of stone slabs run along both sides of them. There are many superb buildings in Saint-Petersburg. In the evening the beautiful deserted city appeared to me as a panoramic work of art in the half-light which differed from the daylight and nightlight and washed everything in a magic illumination.

Sophie Choiseul-Gouffier

The Admiralty as rebuilt by the architect Zakharov is a splendid structure now, a landmark adorning the city… A marvelous boulevard of lime trees surrounds it… An excellent site for sightseeing from which one can see everything magnificent and beautiful in Saint-Petersburg…

Konstantin Batyushkov

I kept on walking in the same direction and soon saw the great palace of the Admiralty. A thin gilded spire topped by a boat-shaped weather-cock extended from the roof of the tower built as a temple with small pillars. The spire can be seen from a large distance and I noticed it when I was out at the Gulf of Finland. It was late autumn but the trees in the alleys surrounding the Admiralty were still in leaves.

Théophile Gautier

43

The passers-by are jostling idly,
All dressed in their Sunday best,
The crowds push ahead so wildly,
The feathered hats attract the epaulets..

　　　　Nikolai Ogarev

...You have seen the Sennaya Square and the Gorokhovaya Street, you have seen how their dirty markets, their dark alleyways, their incessant noisy traffic, their lively colorful crowds of the common people living through their busy working lives, their rough kind features, the cab-drivers, street hawkers, children, charwomen, and workmen speaking in their coarse shrill voices. This is what serves the people in place of the Nevsky Prospekt; in the latter there is interest for news, connections, expenses, notoriety, and entertainment, in the former there is a search for rest, work, bread and drink.

　　Aleksandr Bashutsky

We were amazed with the wonderful wooden pavement on the Nevsky Prospekt along which the carriages seemed to be gliding.

　　Clara Schumann

45

The Nevsky Prospekt begins at the Admiralty Square and continues for a long distance reaching the walls of the Monastery of Saint Aleksandr Nevsky where it curves and ends... The Admiralty spire resembling a mast of golden ship perched on the top of a Greek temple is wonderfully positioned in the perspective of the long avenue. It glitters even under a weak sunlight and the gleam gladdens your eye wherever you can see it...
Both sides of the avenue are lined with wide and tall buildings that look like palaces and rich townhouses... It is a wonderful architectural ensemble and the appellation of "prospect" or avenue given to it as to many other streets in Saint-Petersburg seems to be very fitting to reality, in my opinion. Everything is suited to produce an optical effect and the city that was created as if at once by a will that knew no holds, rising up ready-made from the swamps. As if a scenery machinist gave a whistle and the scene was changed in a theater.

Théophile Gautier

*The graceful towers and castles
Are crowding the busy streets
Along the river banks…*

        Aleksandr Pushkin

46

...We visited the Kazan Cathedral of a somewhat peculiar design; a semicircular row of columns opens the entrance to the church. A massive silver iconostasis in the cathedral is a gift of the Cossacks who seized from the invading French troops the silver utensils stolen by them from the Russian churches.

   Friedrich Hagern

I have also viewed the splendid Church of Our Lady of Kazan; its exterior is magnificent and noble while silver and gold in the interior blind you with their glitter; you may imagine you have penetrated the Temple of the Sun that existed in Lima in the past.

   Sophie Choiseul-Gouffier

47

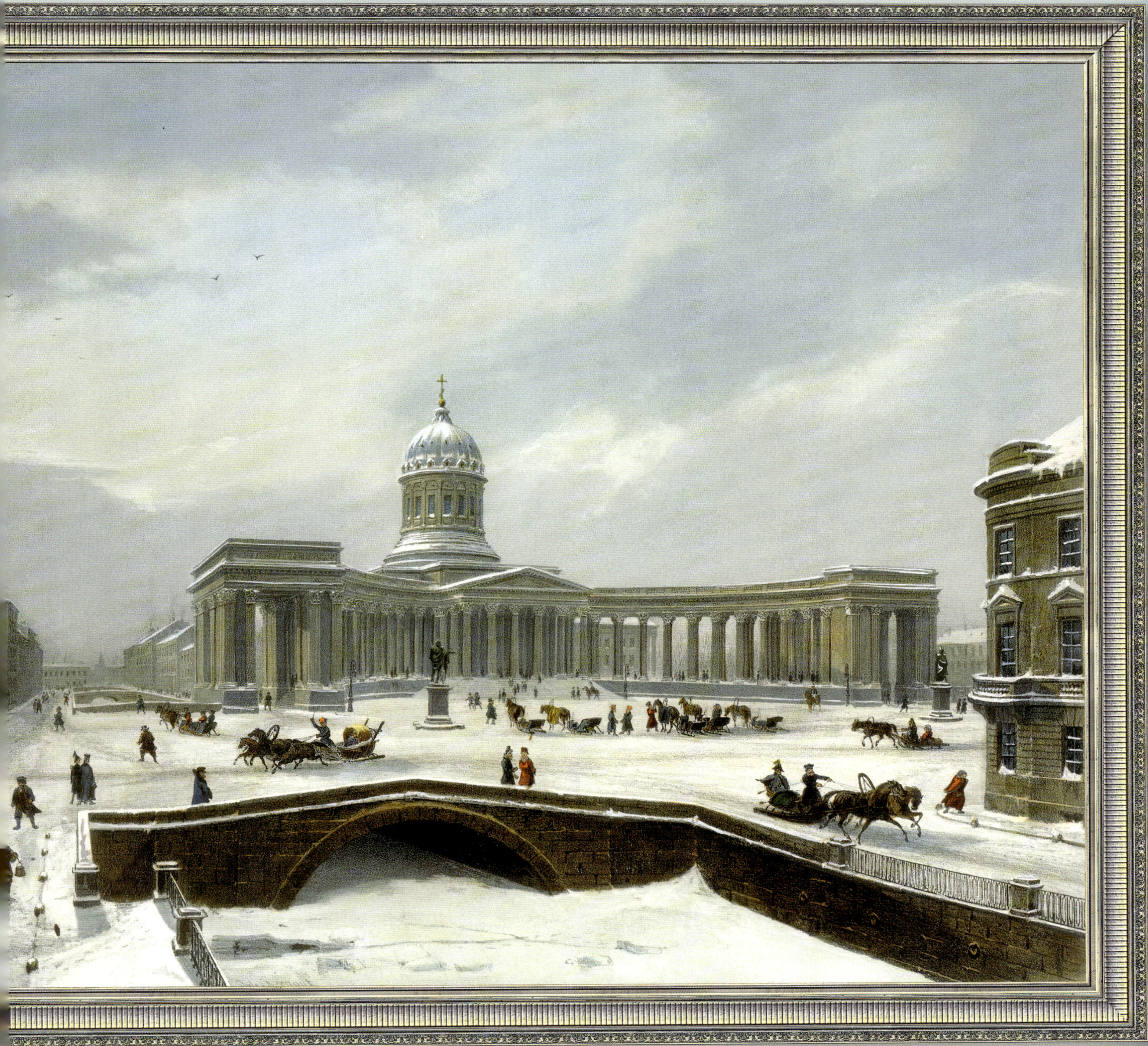

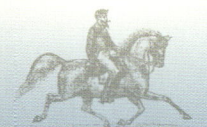

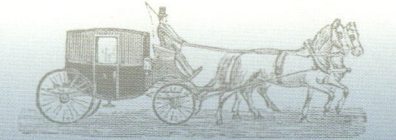

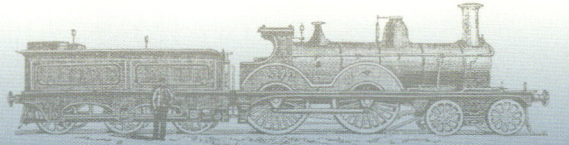

The rigid simplicity of the outline of Saint Isaac's Cathedral immediately indicates that though its design seems so well-integrated it includes elements of an earlier church that had been so successfully incorporated into it. It was a church in honor of the same saint which was successively improved by Peter the Great, Catherine II, and Pavel I though it was not completed to perfection by neither of them... Looking from a corner of the Admiralty Square one can see the Saint Isaac's Cathedral in all its glory. One can judge the building as a whole from that point of view as one sees fully the main façade, one of the side porticos and three of the four smaller cupolas. The large gilded dome on a pillared rotunda is topped with a tolus and a cross and glitters against the open sky.

Théophile Gautier

I was greatly amazed with the bridge here which was laid over boats supporting it; crowds of bearded men and dressed-up women go over it, carriages driven by six or seven horses go over it at such a distance from each other that there seems to be many more of them.

Martha Wilmot

I stood near the river,
It was a frosty foggy night,
I saw Saint Isaac's throwing light,
Its golden dome a-glimmer.

Fedor Tyutchev

51

In winter the wheels are removed from the carriages to be replaced with sleds. Traveling by sleighs over the wide smooth winter roads is always marvelous because the roads are even as if packed with the finest sand; nothing can be faster than the speed with which you ride or, better to say, glide along the roads of this spectacular city.

Louis Philippe de Ségure

> The sleigh of the Tsar slides in the street
> Pulled by powerful horses
> In silver-buckled harness...
> He is immovable, looking ahead
> As snow flakes keep flashing fast,
> The hood of his coat is hiding his head,
> Rustled by the wind rushing past.
>
> *Nikolai Simborsky*

*A famous city stands
On the banks of a glorious river...
It's famous in Northern lands
For its culture and learning that glitter
And traders who grow and prosper.*

        Nikolai Yazykov

The three-level building of the library faces the Nevsky Prospekt on one side and the Gostiny Dvor arcade of shops on the other side. Its central part is decorated with a frontispiece of Doric columns topped with huge statues of the Greek philosophers and the gilded inscription *Imperial Public Library*. Each Tuesday the library was open for visitors from 11 in the morning until 2 in the afternoon.

        Pavel Svinyin

The onrush of people is the greatest between one and two in the afternoon; in addition to the passers-by who are hurrying along the streets there come other people just taking a walk whose only purpose is to show themselves, to look at other people and stretch their legs for a while. In case they decide to continue going in a carriage, their coaches are following behind them along the pavement or awaiting them at a prearranged place.

Théophile Gautier

55

56

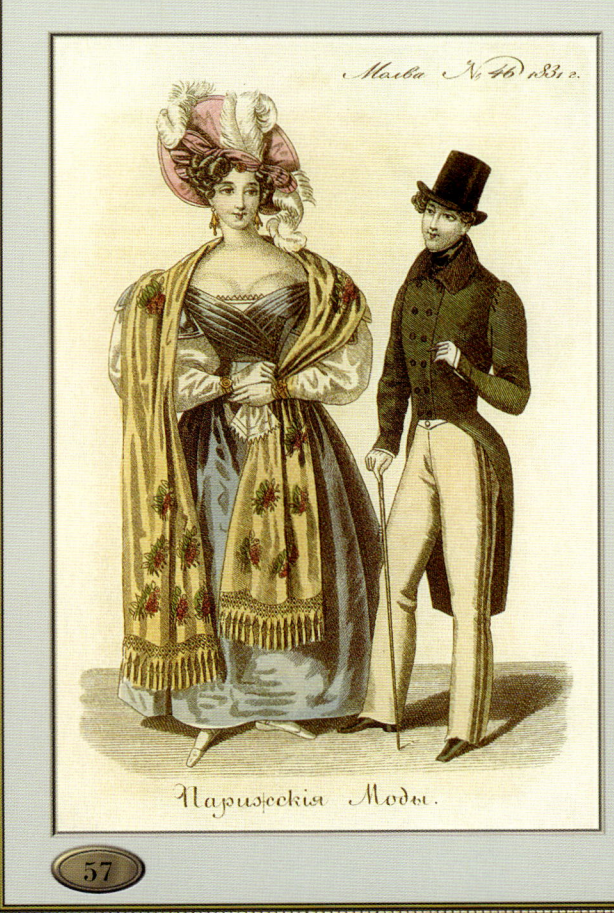

57

Парижскія Моды.

The Bolshoy Theater or the Italian Opera is magnificent, it is extremely large and can be compared to "La Scala" or "San Carlo" theaters... As in the Royal Theater in London the members of the public do not appear in the Saint-Petersburg theater without a frock coat, white neckerchief, and straw-colored or other light-colored gloves; otherwise military or civilian uniforms are allowed which are especially common here. Ladies are in the evening décolleté dresses with bare arms. Such are the society customs and I like them. They contribute significantly to the performance success.

Théophile Gautier

Saint-Catherine's (Smolny) Institute consists of two houses each include one hundred and fifty maidens from the gentry and merchant families; their education is guided by the Empress herself who ensures that they receive everything that a rich family can provide for their daughters. Even the least details of the Institute life are distinguished with order and elegance while the teaching of fine arts is based on religion and moral principles...

Louise Germaine de Staël

The monastery with its church and tombs is one of the miracles of Russia.

Astolphe de Custine

Many noblemen erected monuments to their ancestors in the graveyard of the Aleksandro-Nevskaya Lavra monastery.

Louise Germaine de Staël

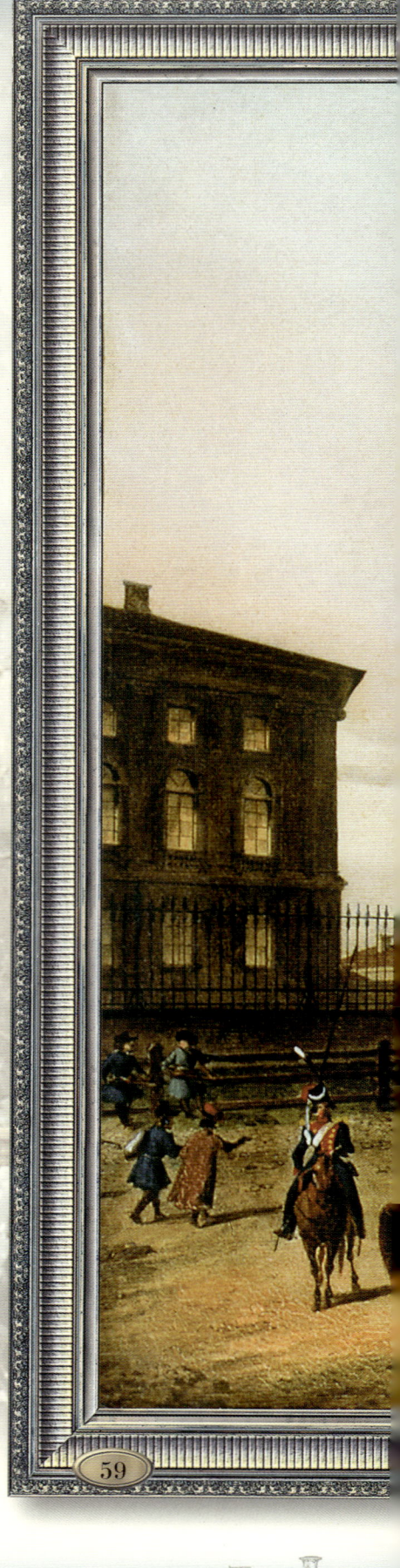

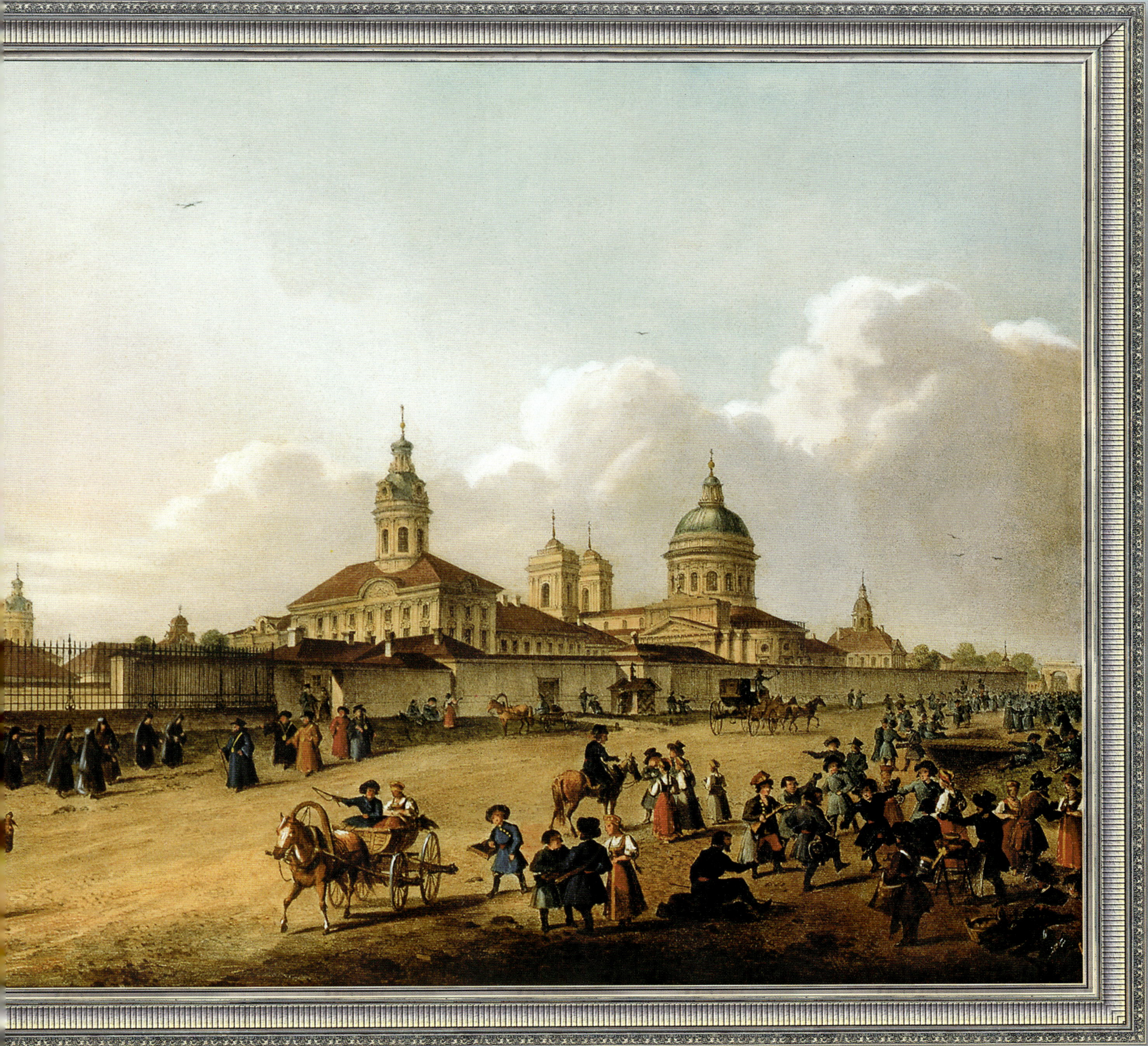

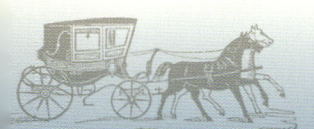

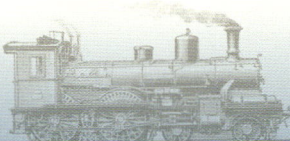

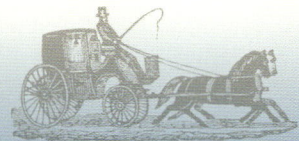

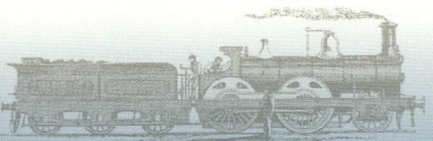

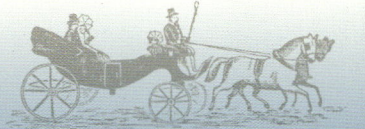

60

*I love the luxurious belt of the islands
And the slender grace of the Petersburg lands.*
Petr Vyazemsky

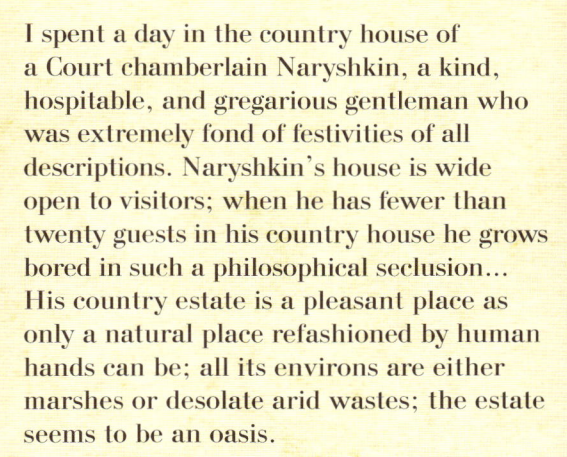

I spent a day in the country house of a Court chamberlain Naryshkin, a kind, hospitable, and gregarious gentleman who was extremely fond of festivities of all descriptions. Naryshkin's house is wide open to visitors; when he has fewer than twenty guests in his country house he grows bored in such a philosophical seclusion... His country estate is a pleasant place as only a natural place refashioned by human hands can be; all its environs are either marshes or desolate arid wastes; the estate seems to be an oasis.

Louise Germaine de Staël

The Islands is nothing else but a huge park with numerous villas and cottages which serves as a substitution of the countryside for the inhabitants of Saint-Petersburg, a resting place for the courtiers that is densely populated during the short summer season and deserted in other seasons. Several very picturesque roads are leading there over several bridges across various river branches.

Astolphe de Custine

I hurried to the Bolshaya Morskaya Street to the department of mail stagecoaches and while waiting for the coach departure I kept on admiring the magnificent charming house which was recently built for the department. The splendid well-lit spacious foyer, the common waiting room for passengers furnished with excellent settees, carpets, mirrors and rich furniture, in short, everything was tastefully arranged and exquisite in quality, all provisions were made for the comfort and repose of the passengers. The arrangements for passenger comforts are so elaborate that even the courtyard where passengers are boarding the carriages is topped with a glass roof.

"Severnaya Pchela", 1848

Prince Mikhail Vorontsov who had lived abroad for a long time established the mail stagecoach service in that year. The government started construction work on the highway in the same period. The enterprise started by Vorontsov was warmly supported by the public and on September 1, 1820, the first stagecoach carrying seven passengers, men and women of different ranks, started on its way to Moscow from the stagecoach department building in the Bolshaya Morskaya Street.

Mikhail Pylyaev

The bulky stagecoach looks eerie
On a Russian highway dreary,
Not as a German primly dressed
On a German road blessed.

Petr Vyazemsky

62

63

Departure from Saint-Petersburg, winter of 1858. A Russian railroad train consists of several linked cars connected by doors between them any of which passengers may open or close as they desire. Each car looks as an apartment with a foyer where the hand luggage is stored and where a toilet room is. The entrance foyer opens into a small exposed platform enclosed with railings to which a passenger can climb from outside over a ladder which is obviously much more convenient than steps in our cars.

65

66

Wood-burning stoves heat the air in the cars up to fifteen—sixteen degrees. The windows are lined at the sides with felt strips which prevent cold air from penetrating into the car and keep the air warm inside. You see that in January you are traveling from Saint-Petersburg to Moscow in an atmosphere which is far from the Arctic cold while a Parisian would tremble when just hearing of such a cold...

Théophile Gautier

The bell has rung the end of lengthy journey,
The mighty engine breathing hard with smoke
Has stopped before him, weary and heavy.

Aleksei Apukhtin

The passengers premises of the first and second classes are built very well of stone, bricks and cast iron, the 30-feet wide rooms have boldly designed and strongly built vaulted roofs, the galleries are supported by cast iron pillars, the platforms are laid with granite slabs and generally the buildings look quite impressive.

Anton Stuckenberg

A wide settee stretches along the wall of the first compartment of the car; it is intended for those who would like to sleep and for the people who are used to sit down in a cross-legged Oriental fashion. I preferred to sit on a soft overstuffed chair in the second compartment and cozily arranged myself in a corner. I found myself in a wheeled home and no hardships of the carriage travel were threatening me. I could stand up, walk around from one compartment to another with that freedom of movement that is familiar to the passengers of steamships and which is not known to the miserable traveler imprisoned in a stagecoach, a mail carriage, or in such a railroad car as they are still furnished in France.

Théophile Gautier

68

69

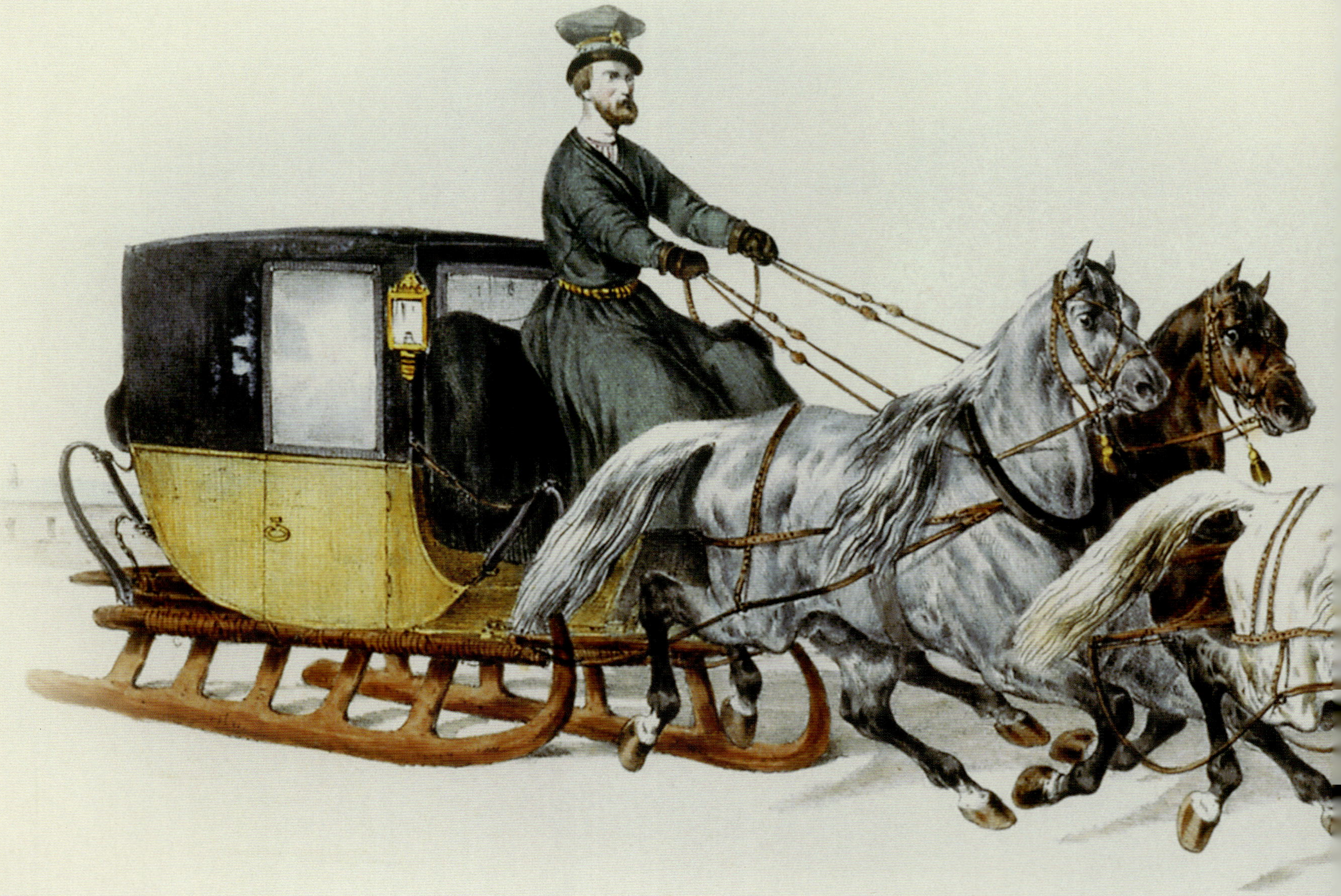

"In carriage, in sledge or on foot…"

In Russia all distances are long: there is nothing but distances in those bare expanses stretching as far as eye can see: the two or three sites worth visiting are at distances of hundreds of leagues from each other.

Astolphe de Custine

70

The city slips away as magic dream,
The evergreens in islands, houses and spires—
All disappear rapidly behind us…
   Fedor Glinka

71

Ekateringof and the Krestovsky Island are the most popular recreation sites to which the city dwellers flock for amusement and picnics. One can go there in a coach or in a boat.
   François Ancelot

The bridges have pretty latticed railings decorated with the Emperor's coat of arms; they are supported by the square granite pillars which rush before the eyes of the astounded traveler as wild visions in the mind of a fevered patient.
   Astolphe de Custine

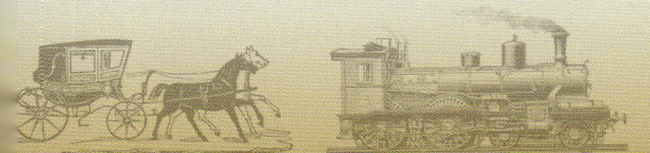

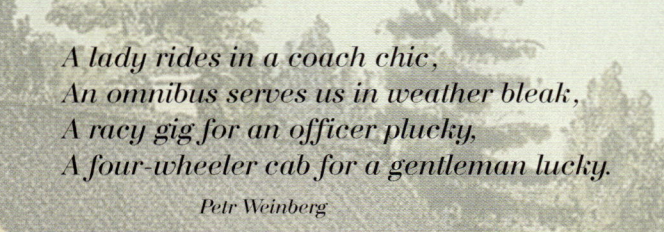

A lady rides in a coach chic,
An omnibus serves us in weather bleak,
A racy gig for an officer plucky,
A four-wheeler cab for a gentleman lucky.

Petr Weinberg

72

73

The fashion or custom in Saint-Petersburg commands everybody who is not an absolute pauper to move out to a country home in summer, to breathe in the damp airs of the marshes in the mornings and evenings and in the day time, instead of relaxing in shade, to breathe dust on the pavements while running around the shops or on business errands, and to spend the nights with the crawling, jumping, and flying insects, permanent inhabitants of the cheap rental countryside cottages and the wet woods.

"Severnaya Pchela", 1834

The yesterday's entertainment at Ekateringof was marked by public appearance of the Omnibus. Two excellent carriages filled with passengers each driven by four superb horses were riding in the city even before the event. The carriages are elegant and comfortable and neatly kept. The interior of an omnibus is divided into two compartments, each accommodating up to six persons sitting on soft cushions face to face, three in a row. Up to twelve persons can be accommodated on the top of the carriage. The passers-by stopped and stared in the streets when they saw these extraordinary vehicles. Everybody approve the new notion and wish the enterprise success. The inventive Russians are finding new, more familiar and funny appellations for the foreign contraption.

"Severnaya Pchela", 1830

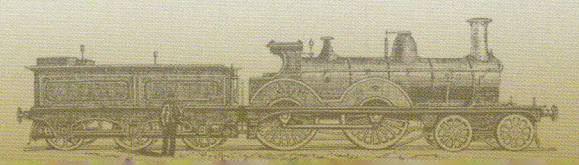

74

The area of Petergof presents the most wonderful sight of natural beauty that I have seen so far in Russia. A low craggy shore overhangs the sea that starts directly at the fringe of the park approximately a third of a league below the palace built at the edge of the low hill that descends almost vertically down; very comfortable downward paths have been built into this natural steep hill side; you are descending from one terrace to another one to a park where you see very large and shady groves of cultivated trees and shrubs.

Astolphe de Custine

Then we went to a small house or a pavilion called "Mon Plaisir" which was built by Peter the Great at the sea shore. A veranda has been built looking onto the shore and a breakfast table is laid on a platform set under a large tree... The park ensemble is magnificent and nothing else can be imaginable as a more appropriate evidence of the glory of the Emperor that preserves a memory of him.

Francisco Miranda

At one time I kept on asking for assistance in surveying the cottage of the Emperor and the Empress. It is a small house they built in a neo-Gothic style according to the English fashion. It is located deep into the splendid Petergof park.

Astolphe de Custine

The sun is sprinkling sea with gold!
The day is blooming and the cold
Water is like silver mirror capturing the light!

Fedor Glinka

*O blessed Pavlovsk, my love for your parks
Is endless, O heaven and haven of dreams!*

Emile Dupré de Saint-Maure

Now the favorite sites for promenading are the Nevsky Prospekt, the Neva embankments, and the Summer Garden. Soon the public will be rushed by the invisible steam power with the speed of an arrow to Tsarskoe Selo or Pavlovsk to breathe there a better air than in the low-lying city.

Franz Gerstner

Visualize an immense building built in a semi-circle with open galleries, magnificent rooms and numerous separate chambers, very comfortable and quiet... A grand hall artfully designed by the architect Andrei Stakenschneider, who built the railway station, is decorated with oblong pillars, a spacious balcony and a highly intricate fountain, it is filled with tables and accommodates two luxurious bars.

Nestor Kukolnik

The Eastern bank is lit by setting sun,
The palace of the tsars seems guilded by the light,
Like somber giant, when the day is done,
Is looking lonely into a mirror bright.

Vasily Zhukovsky

81

82

When I arrived at Tsarskoe Selo the Empress was so kind that she herself was showing me the beauties of her magnificent suburban palace. Clear streams, shady green, graceful pavilions, impressive buildings, the most excellent furniture, and the rooms lined with porphyry, malachite or lazulite all blended into a magical sight and looked like Armida's palaces and gardens for an amazed traveler.

Louis Philippe de Ségure

83

90

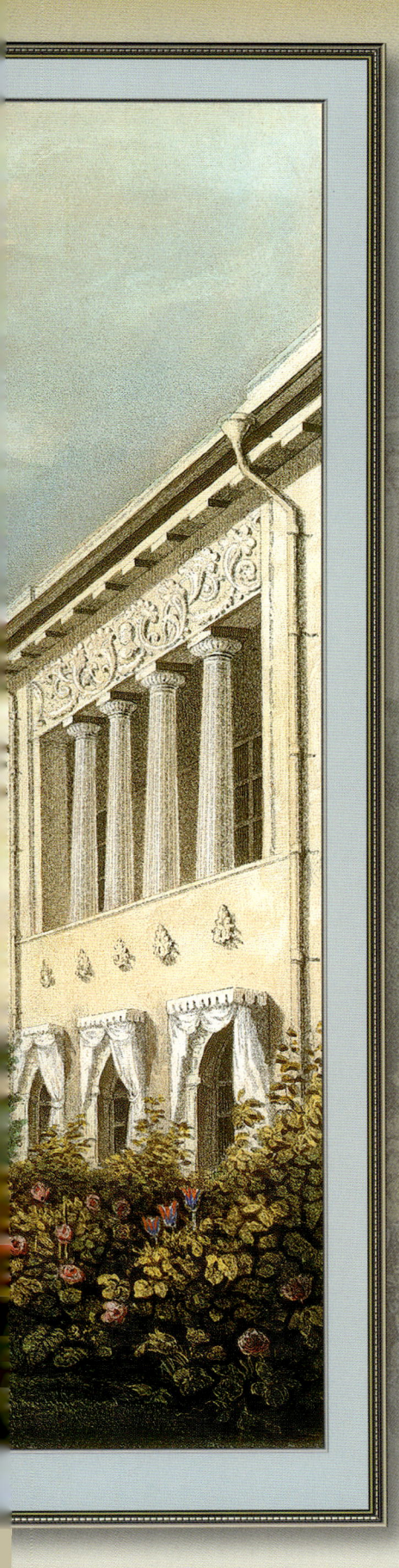

I should like to have a design of a classical house planned as it was done in antiquity… I would be able to build such a Greco-Roman rhapsody in My Tsarskoe Selo garden.
Catherine II

When entering the park we cannot help admiring the wonderful Ionic arcade erected by Cameron near the palace. The colonnade looks magnificent and buoyant at the same time, it is a veritable masterpiece of exquisite taste crowned with flowers blooming in hanging gardens on top of it. Catherine gave an order to place busts of great persons of all ages and nations between the columns.
François Ancelot

To travel by a mail stagecoach service from Saint-Petersburg to Moscow is to live through full days of the sensations one feels when going for the carnival rides in Paris known as the "Russian rides". It would be worthwhile to bring to Saint-Petersburg an English carriage if only for having the privilege of riding a carriage with a really good suspension (in the Russian coaches the suspension is merely an appellation) along that famous highway which the Russians and, I think foreigners, too, call the best highway in Europe. Indeed, it is maintained well but the surface is paved with gravel that is so hard that the screws in the carriage body are readily loosened by bumping and one or two screws are invariably lost while you are traveling from one mail station to another. Therefore, at the station you will waste the time you gained while rushing at a breakneck speed in clouds of dust to reach the station.

Astolphe de Custine

The Russian coachman is sitting on a high driver's seat and transfers the leading reins from one hand to another and seems to be absolutely fearless. Even on the most terrible of roads he can force the foursome under his control to gallop spurring his stallions to the fullest speed just by yelling and extremely rarely using the whip hanging from his arm.

François Ancelot

*You will not feel the painful bumps,
As you will ride a-flying;
You'll fail to sense the heavy jumps,
As you'll enjoy your crying*

Petr Vyazemsky

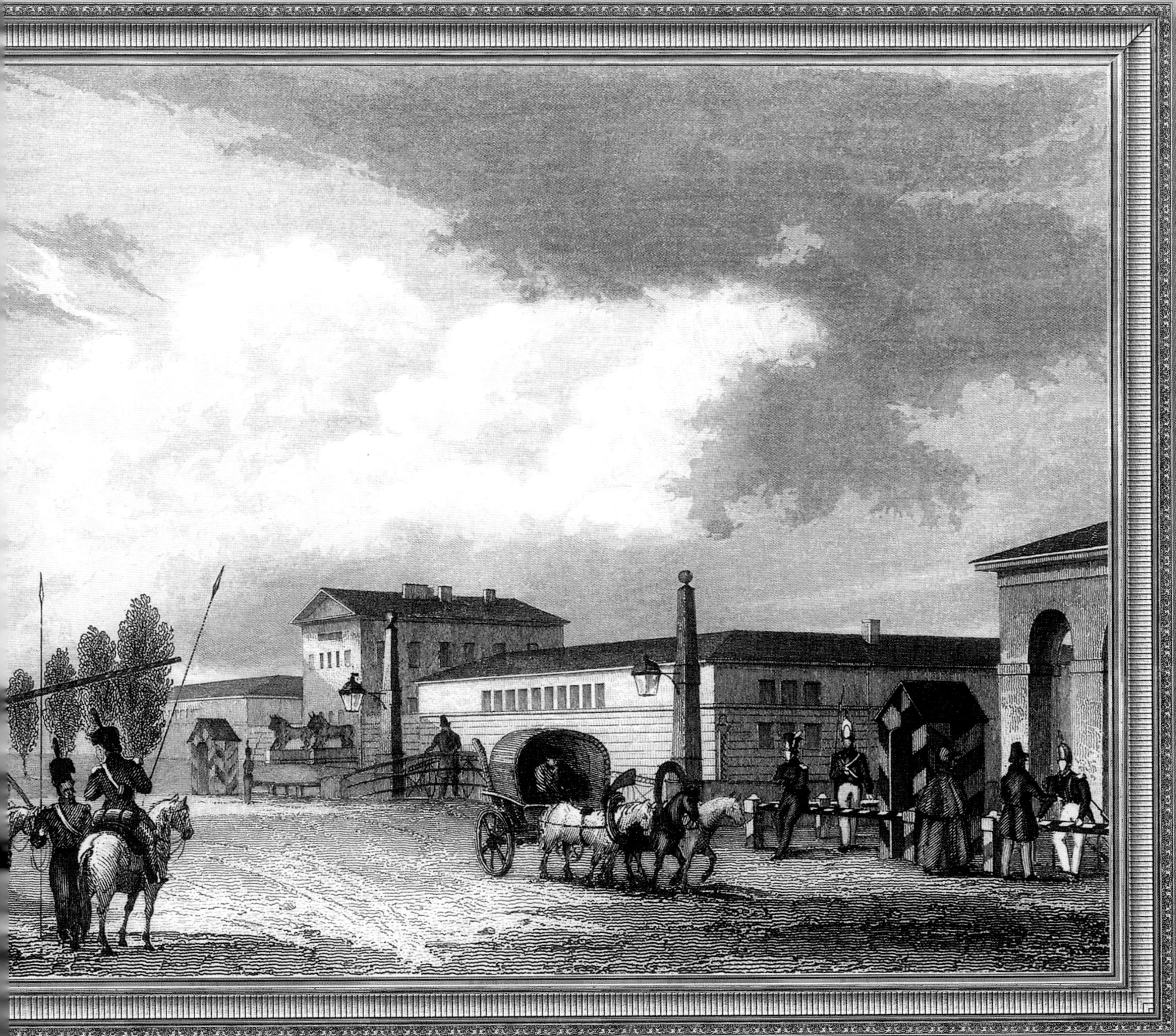

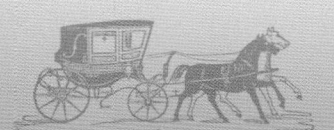

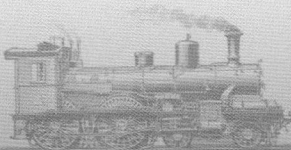

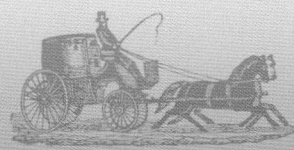

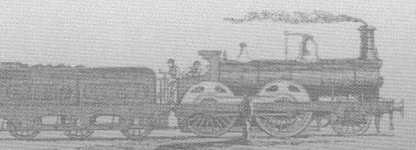

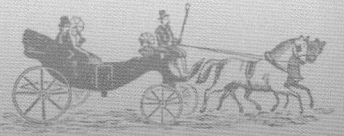

94

*...paved roads will traverse Russia's length
bringing her unity and strength;
and iron bridges will go arching
over the waters in a sweep;
mountains will part; below the deep,
audacious tunnels will be marching:
God-fearing folk will institute
an inn at each stage of the route.*

Aleksandr Pushkin

Team of three fast horses carried me on over the newly built splendid highway paved with stone which is laid according to the new plan of the Empress who desired that the entire road to Saint-Petersburg had to be the same; they are building stone bridges and other magnificent structures but there is still not a single mail stage post with an inn here...

Francisco Miranda

Traveling is very strenuous because the roads are unbelievably bad, there is nothing they can be compared to. My coach has literally disintegrated into atoms, not a single piece of glass was left intact in it. Now I have to wait before they install new sleds to the coach (the old sleds have broken down into small pieces). I am traveling day and night and can boast of being capable of sleeping under any circumstances. Yesterday the coach broke down and they repaired it while I was sleeping. The road quality is too terrible to describe.

Martha Wilmot

91

The rich gentlemen traveled with veritable convoys; a journey from Saint-Petersburg to Moscow was a challenging and strenuous endeavor because the roads with their potholes, sand drifts, and log pavements were in a very poor state at that time.

Mikhail Pylyaev

The merry voice of carriage bell
Was carried far and wide,
It could be heard in distant dell
And then was left behind.

Petr Vyazemsky

Having traveled some distance I noticed that the surrounding sights are starting to change: hills and glades have appeared, we could see houses constructed of thicker logs. I asked my servant and the mail coachman ("izvozchik") what was the price of such a house a variety of which could be bought in any village and they answered that the usual price varied between only twenty and twenty four rubles.

Francisco Miranda

Before starting on a journey a rich gentleman sent ahead of him a team of cooks with a full set of cooking implements and a store of provisions. In towns arrangements were made to stay overnight at the houses of acquaintances or wealthy local merchants. In villages the servants selected a cleaner peasant dwelling and decorated it with the carpets and curtains brought with them. The gentleman's family with children left for the road later accompanied by wet nurses, companions, governesses and the entire train took seven or eight days to reach Moscow.

Mikhail Pylyaev

What can I tell you about my trip? It continues under the most favorable manifestations with the exception of the appalling road and the dreadful coachmen. Bumping, elbow nudges, and so on are greatly distressing to my two companions; I am begging their pardon for the discomforts but when traveling together people must forgive each other for some things.

Aleksandr Pushkin

The Russian coachman seems at first sight to be an Oriental as he is dressed in a thick broadcloth coat or in a colored shirt of homespun linen similar to the Greek chiton. The Russians are reining only from the coach driver's seat unless the coach is very heavy or is driven by six or eight horses but even in the latter case the coachman sits in front of the coach. The coachman holds in his hands a thick bundle of reins consisting of eight straps controlling four horses harnessed in a row. His elegance and dexterity, his speed and diligence with which he controls the picturesque horse team, the very gracefulness of all his movements, the agility with which he jumps down from the coach, his supple body, and ultimately his entire bearing reminds one of the most graceful peoples in the world.

Astolphe de Custine

*The coachman drives on with flair
Into a village on a holiday,
He tips his hat to maidens fair,
He looks so keen and very gay.*

Petr Vyazemsky

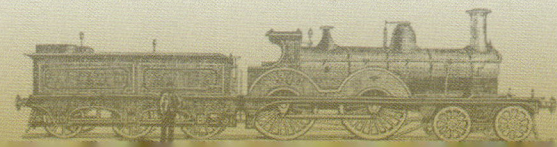

96

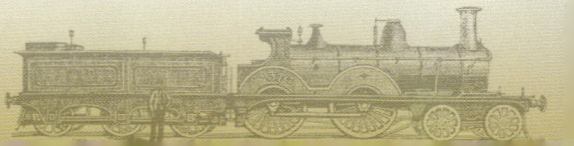

I was passing through Novgorod and many thoughts flashed in my brain — ancient Slavs, Princes Ryurik, Vadim, and Aleksandr Nevsky… I recalled Saint Vladimir who baptized Russia into the Greek Christian faith, I recalled his grandfather Dobrynya, I could not forget the rallying bell whose ringing could bring to arms from 40 to 100 thousand warriors ready to enter a bloody battle, nor the city ruler Isaac Boretsky and glorious Lady Marfa, and the tsar Ioann the Terrible…

Gavriyl Gerakov

Novgorod is divided by the very beautiful Volkhov River into two parts known as the Trading area and the Sofyiskaya area where the Saint Sophia Cathedral stands. The areas are connected by a bridge built of bricks and timber.

Francisco Miranda

97

At last we arrived at Novgorod having covered 35 more versts. It is a very ancient large city. Most houses are wooden and built in the old Russian style. The city is ringed with high adobe walls with numerous ancient towers; there are very many churches in the city.

Francisco Miranda

98

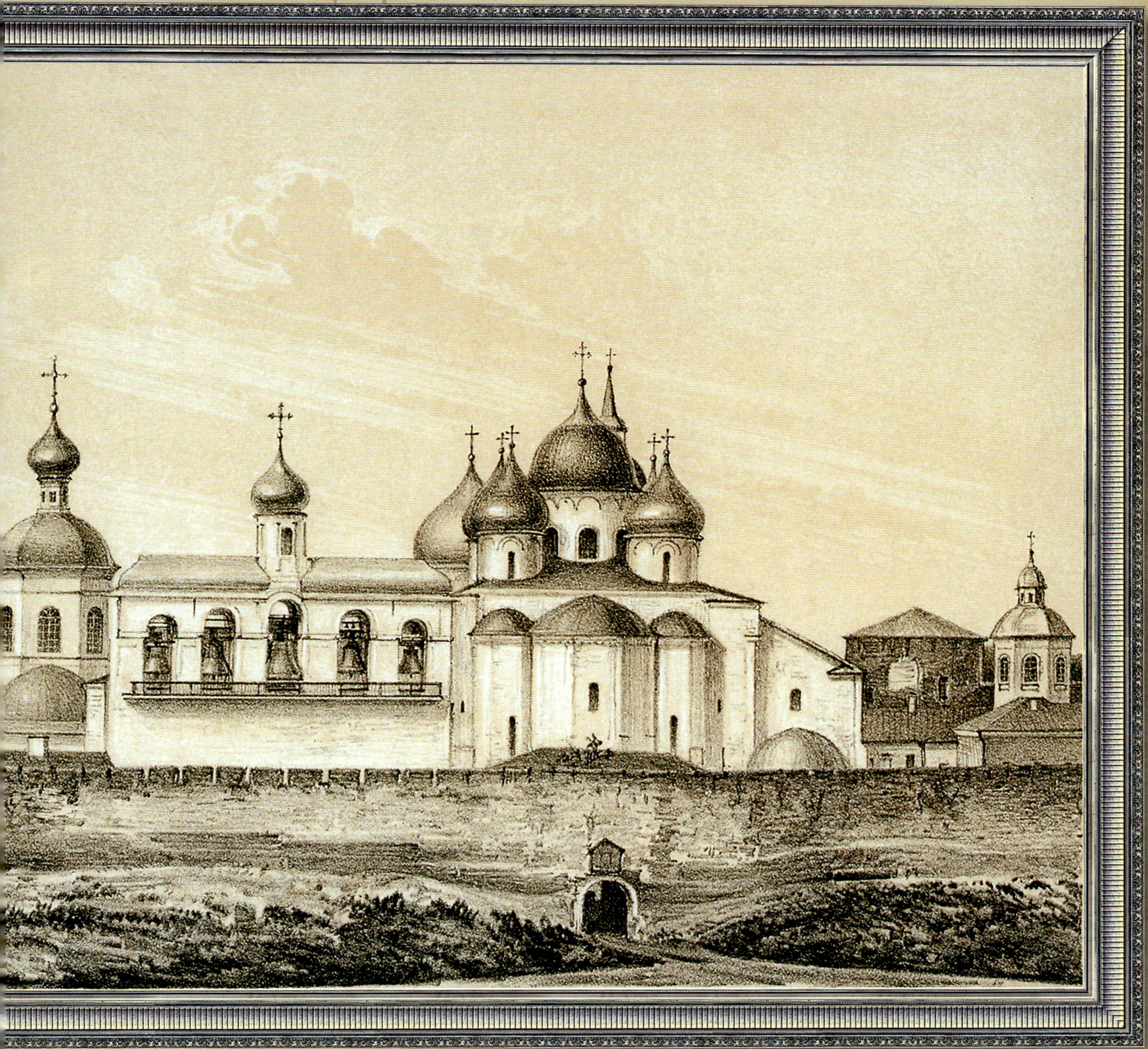

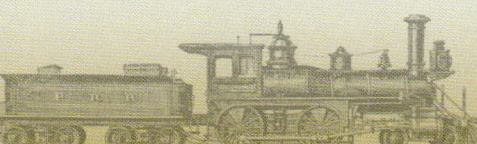

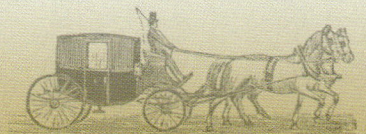

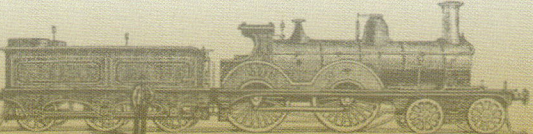

Видъ сѣверозападной стороны.

Первокласснаго святоозерскаго Иверскаго Богородицкаго Монастыря состоящаго на островѣ Валдайскаго Озера близь города Валдая въ которомъ имѣется Чудотворный образъ Пресвятыя Богородицы Иверскія отъ Афонскія горы принесенный и Святаго Праведнаго Іакова мощи на- -крытіи почиваютъ и части Святыхъ мощей Петра Алексѣя Іоны и Филиппа Митрополитовъ Московскихъ и всея Росси Чудотворцевъ

по Благословенію Высокопреосвященнѣйшаго Серафима Митрополита Новгородскаго, Санктпетербургскаго, Эстляндскаго и Финляндскаго, и разныхъ орденовъ Кавалера
Усердіемъ настоятеля обители сея Архимандрита Герасима Гайдукова съ братіею 1824 Года

Описаніе имѣющагося строенія.

1е Соборная церковь Успенія Божія матери 2е Тёплая двухэтажная церковь въ низу Бого- -явленія Господня и предѣлъ Преподобнаго Нила столобенскаго въ верху Святаго Духа 3е обще- братственная трапеза со службами 4е Больничная церковь Св. Праведнаго Іакова боровицкаго съ больничными келліями 5е Святыя врата 1е надъ которыми церковь Святителя Филиппа Ми- трополита Московскаго 6е внутреннія Соборныя врата надъ которыми церковь Архистратига Михаила 7е Колокольня съ своими часами 8е Настоятельской двухэтажной корпусъ со службами 9е Намѣстническія келліи со службами 10е Братской двухэтажной корпусъ со службами 11е двухэтажной кор- пусъ Гостинныхъ келій для богомольцевъ 12е Башня называемая Патріаршая 13е Скотной дворъ 14е де- ревянной торосъ или ледникъ 15е Братская деревянная баня 16е Настоятельской садъ съ фруктовыми деревами.

99

> The Volkhov River is amazing in that it does not allow itself to be frozen even in the most intense frost as today owing to its swift flow as if it is reminding to all and sundry about the former great Novgorod, about its supremacy and power of old when foreigners used to say that nobody could resist against Lord God and the Great Novgorod…
>
> *Gavriyl Gerakov*

> The old chronicles tell us that Novgorod was ruled by the people. Even though the people had princes ruling them their power was weak. The rule was primarily exercised through people's representatives. The absolute and genuine ruler was the people and the rule was implemented by means of general popular assemblies. The city of Novgorod was ruling the areas far to the North even beyond the Volga River. This free city-state was a member of the Hansa Union of European cities. The power of the city was founded on the trade. The internal dissent and the avaricious neighbor brought it to ruin.
>
> *Aleksandr Radishchev*

> We had dinner in Novgorod, at a very pleasant inn with walls decorated with superb English engravings. In my opinion, no other inn in Russia can be compared to this one in comfort.
>
> *Martha Wilmot*

102

103

The horses kept pushing ahead. The wind kept on steadily increasing in force meanwhile. The tiny puff in sky grew into a huge white cloud, growing, rising, and gradually engulfing the entire heavens. It started snowing finely but suddenly large snow flakes gushed down in droves. The wind was howling and a snow storm has started. Instantaneously the dark sky was immersed into a snow sea. Everything disappeared from sight. The coachman cried, "Hey, Sir, we're in danger, it's a blizzard!"

Aleksandr Pushkin

I started the trip at the worst of times… The coachman, though a plucky lad, was overwhelmed with snow and dropped the reins; left to themselves, the horses brought us up to the village and just stopped there.

Gavriyl Gerakov

104

105

> *A coach fast is sliding in the snow,*
> *The road seems boringly long,*
> *The bell is ringing rather low,*
> *Incessant is its plaintive song.*
>
> Aleksandr Pushkin

*Who's the rider? Where from?
How far he has to strive?*

Petr Vyazemsky

Since the nights are all but nonexistent now it is very pleasant to travel without stopping, especially as one can easily read in the coach even at midnight and I often was doing just that. We have traveled 21 versts and arrived at the Bronnitsa village on the Msta River which we crossed over a wooden bridge or, more exactly, a very narrow wooden platform. A cone-shaped hill topped by a stone-walled church stands in a wide valley about two versts before this village from where one has a splendid panoramic view of the entire surrounding area.

Francisco Miranda

To the right of the highway near the Bronnitsa village there is a tall mountain that can bee seen from a large distance though the entire Novgorod area is quite flat. The mountain is a gigantic cone-shaped mound of heaped earth... It is often said that it is a burial place of an ancient very powerful magician or that the hill was piled by the heathen priests for their idolatry services.

Glushkov

107

Just look at the Russian peasant: can one see at least a trace of slavish submissiveness in his bearing and speech? It goes without saying that he is daring and clever. His capacity for learning is a byword. His skillfulness and agility are astounding. A traveler can cross Russia from end to end without knowing a single word in Russian and he is understood everywhere, his requests are granted, he enters into agreements.

Aleksandr Pushkin

It was Sunday and the young people dressed in their holiday best were amusing themselves in various ways. The maidens were moving up and down on the swings, not in the least worried that everybody could see their legs even though all of them were at least fifteen or more… Such are the local customs.

Francisco Miranda

The local peasants favor wide low hats which sit tightly on their heads making them look like mushrooms… Their large footwear is woven of reeds, they manufacture their shoes themselves and tie them to their feet with strings that serve as shoe laces.

Astolphe de Custine

My love for country life seems strange,
The squalid cabins, poor country folk,
I love to see them dancing on the range,
From their drunken songs I will not balk.
'Tis holiday for them, they dance until they drop,
They worked so hard, I'll stay with them till midnight,
I'm happy when they harvest a rich crop,
They need a holiday to make their life seem bright.

Mikhail Lermontov

108

109

110

111

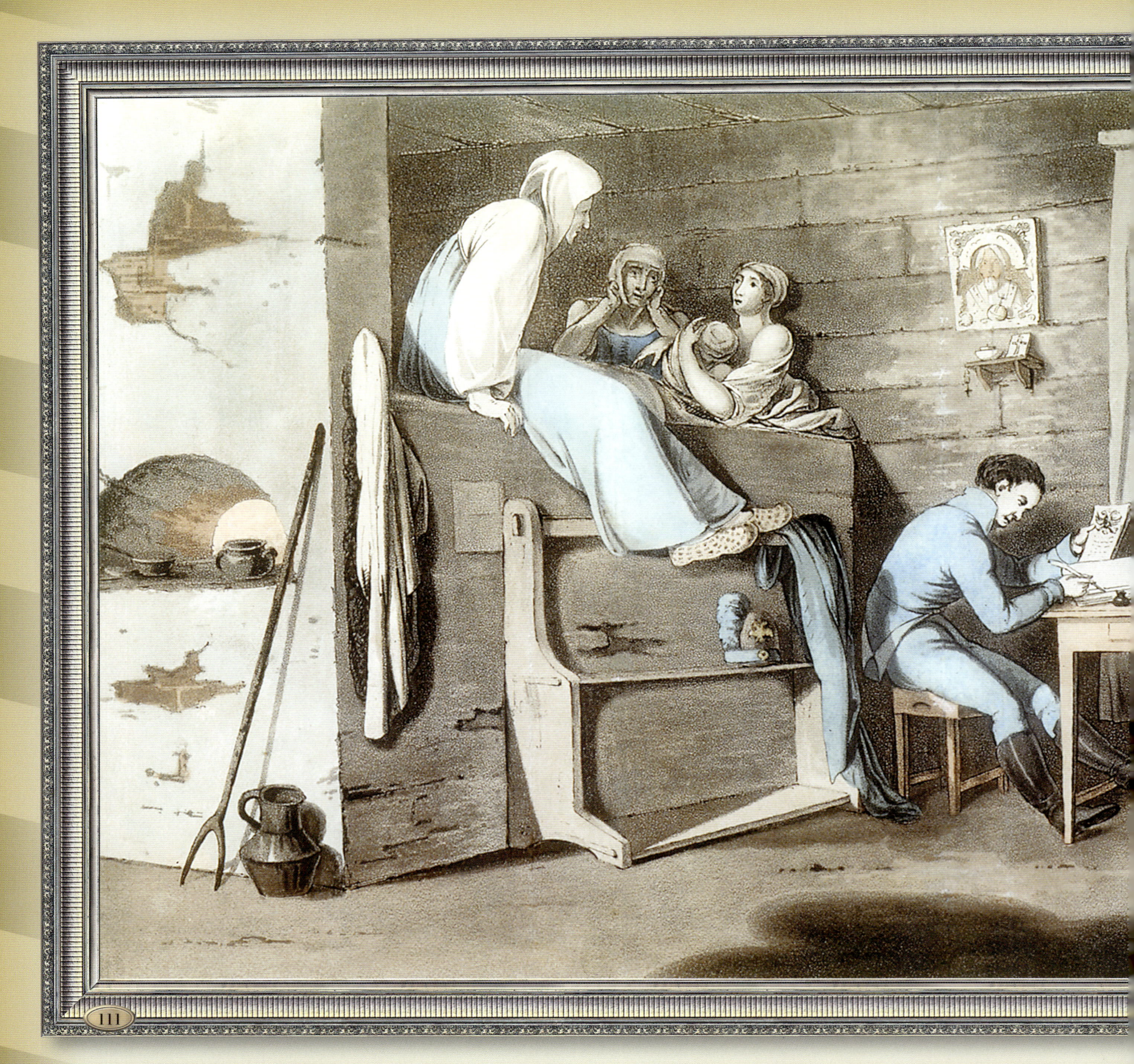

It will not be manor ancestral,
It will not be the churchyard hushed,
The Fate will lay me down at rest
On a highway, busy and rushed.

Aleksandr Pushkin

After traveling 38 versts we arrived at a small town of Kresttsy with agreeable houses in a wide street that started at the very edge of the town from where one obtains a splendid view of the church standing at its end surrounded with lampposts that are lit up at dusk.

Francisco Miranda

I had been tired by the bad road and after leaving the carriage I entered the mail stage cabin hoping to get a rest. I saw there a traveler who was sitting at a long traditional country bench in the front corner looking through some papers and asking the mail stage commissioner for a new change of horses as soon as possible.

Aleksandr Radishchev

They told me much about the Valdai hills which Russians pompously call the Moscow Switzerland. I am approaching Valdai and at a distance of thirty leagues from the town I notice that the area is uneven though not hilly and crisscrossed with shallow ravines where the road is laid down so that the horses continue to run at the same speed at the declines and ascents; they continue going at a high speed but I am still losing time at the post stations where the Russian coachmen are very lazily harnessing horses.

Astolphe de Custine

Valdai is a small town located at one of the most picturesque areas along the route. One might refer to its environs as being romantic and the district is famous for bells and beautiful maidens; the bells emit the sweetest sounds and the maidens have the sweetest faces in this part of the country.

Louis Ricci

It is not true what is told about the Valdai maidens that they surround the passing coaches and carriages throwing cakes at them and crying out, "buy them, buy them!" Nothing of the kind happened to me; I saw several pretty maidens, politely greeted them, said some nice words, bought a few cakes, and perhaps, paid more than they expected. The maidens thanked me, blushed, and even bowed nicely.

Gavriyl Gerakov

*Buy some cakes from pretty maidens
(At Valdai they're very easy)
Then move on without burdens,
You'll find tea so very pleasing.*

Aleksandr Pushkin

Vyshny Volochek is one of the busiest towns between Moscow and Saint-Petersburg because a canal passes through it along which numerous barges are hauled… My carriage broke down and we had to stop at the road… I did not want to waste time and took a seat on the ground at a knoll and made entries into my journal.

Martha Wilmot

The women here are extremely neat… Their clothes are made of various silk fabrics, with some swathing at the back and buttoned down at the front, while rich women have dresses fringed with colored ribbons or with gold lace and passementerie edging.

Glushkov

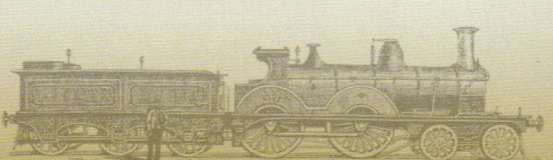

*You'll see few wonders along the gloomy route,
My heart still pines and hopes for its good.*
    Aleksei Apukhtin

The country dwellings resemble archaic ones in their simplicity; they are built of logs knocked together, a small opening is the window, a stove is placed in a narrow room with benches along the walls.

Louis Philippe de Ségure

I have visited several village homes and noticed that they are much more spacious and tidier than the homes in other parts of Russia. I also noted that almost all homes have a handloom to make white linen of the local flax which is used to sew good clothes for the lower classes. I paid 30 kopecks for tea, bread and so on and watched a girl who was milking a cow; she was hiding her face from me but freely exhibited her thighs.

Francisco Miranda

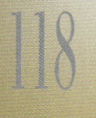

120

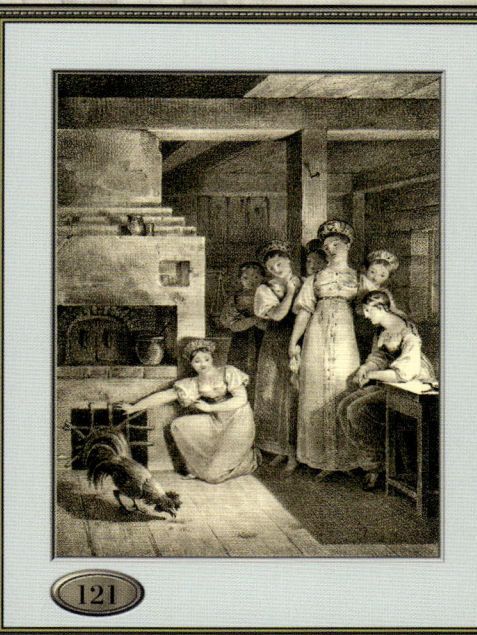

121

When it is unexpectedly seen by a voyager traveling from Saint-Petersburg the town of Torzhok seems to be an encampment built in an open wheat field. Its white houses, towers, and mansions resemble Oriental minarets. One can see guilt spires and cupolas and a variety of bell towers, round and square, tall and low, all green or blue in color some of which are decorated with small columns; in short, this town gives one a foretaste of Moscow. …Torzhok is known for its leather-ware factories that produce handsome well-finished boots, gold- or silver-embroidered shoes very popular with European dandies, in particular those who favor goods brought from distant countries… Torzhok also has another distinctive product, namely, chicken meat balls. When the Emperor visited a small inn in Torzhok he was served amazingly tasty meat balls. Since then the fame of the Torzhok meat balls spread all over Russia.

Astolphe de Custine

In Torzhok I had the pleasure of eating the veal meat balls, the tastiest dish in Europe… Their fame was so great and widespread that the Empress herself was extremely curious and hoped to taste them…

Louis Ricci

In Torzhok find time to eat,
Try meat-balls at Pozharsky's inn,
It's fried chicken (it's a treat),
Then back to highway, strong and lean.

Aleksandr Pushkin

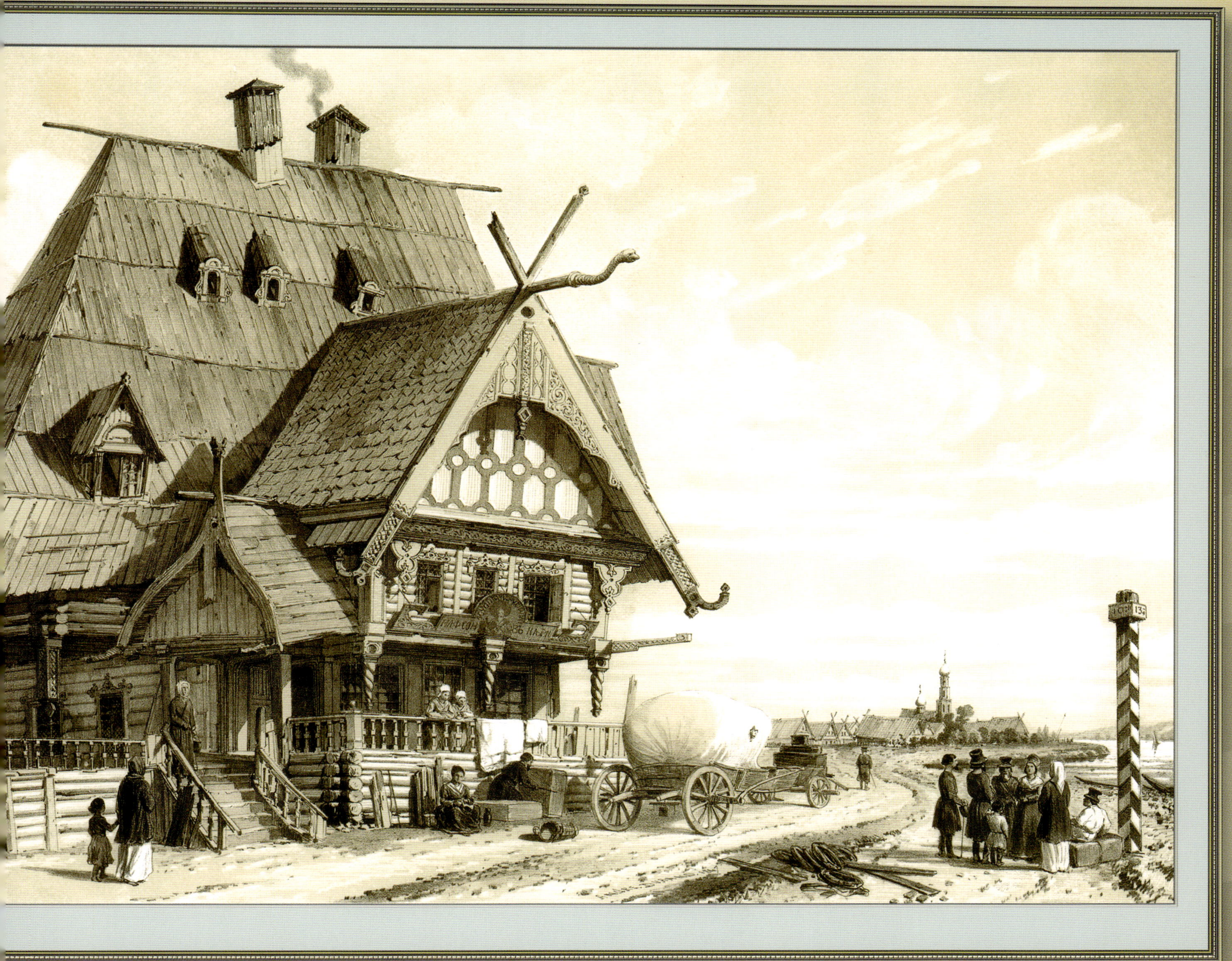

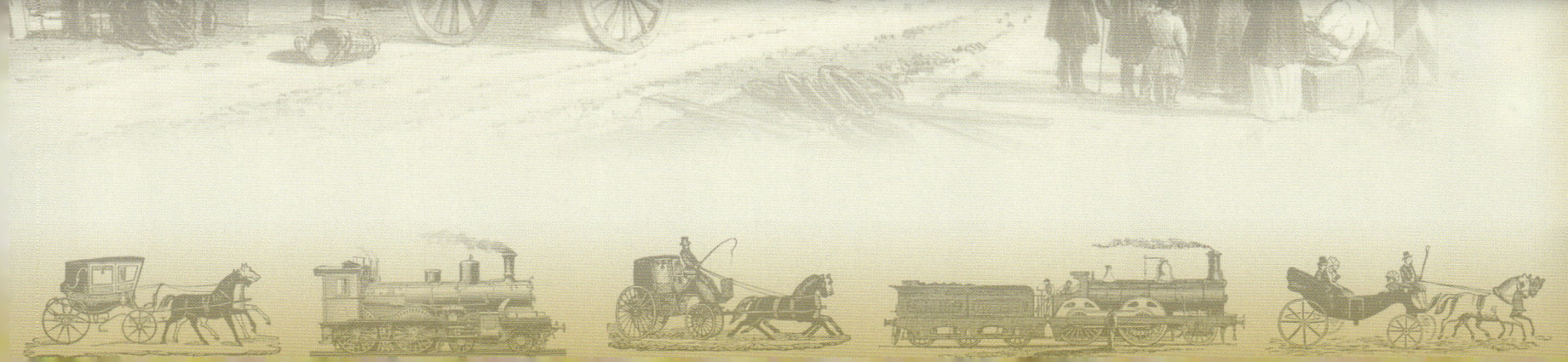

> We saw Tver by the evening against a beautiful sunset. It is a remarkable and extensive city.
>
> *Clara Schumann*

> …When you are entering the city you are witnessing a picturesque scene. At a distance at the end of the avenue you see the curving Volga River; a fortress surrounded with the earth walls is on its bank, further you see the amazingly symmetric and well-balanced embankment behind which you find the tops of the houses, the church cupolas and the bell-tower spires, and finally there is a dark forest of masts of the numerous barges hauling the immense riches from the most distant corners of Russia to the capital of the North.
>
> *Glushkov*

> Another magnificent city is Tver on the Volga River. I left my coach to wash my hands and taste the river water; the great river is not the only proud possession of Tver, this new city is the main city of a province… The local inhabitants wear very colorful clothes which differ very much from the clothes worn in the neighboring provinces.
>
> *Martha Wilmot*

> Tver is a very picturesque city. When you are looking at a crowd of the city and country women in their peculiar head-dresses, necklaces, long white fringed scarves, richly ornamented belts, gold rings, and earrings you can imagine yourself witnessing an ancient Oriental festivity.
>
> *Louis Philippe de Ségure*

...*Valdai, Torzhok and Tver flash by*
As his coach rushes on...
   Aleksandr Pushkin

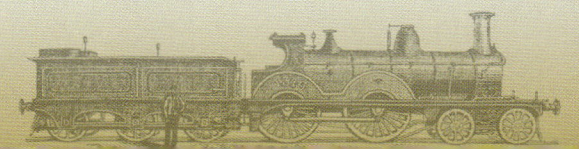

127

This city has numerous solid stone houses. They say that it has as many as ten thousand inhabitants. When I entered the inn, very tidy and cozy, it was heavily raining and rather cold. The paths were sprinkled with sand as they do in Holland and bunches of aromatic herbs were hung in the rooms. I was immediately served some tea and bread and butter for mere 30 kopecks and I continued strolling along the main streets of the city which are rather wide and straight as if they were laid down with a ruler; some of the streets are hard topped. The houses also look fine.

Francisco Miranda

…The city is very neat and Volga makes it look especially attractive. The late Empress was greatly favoring the city of Tver and after the great fire at the end of 1760s in which most of the city burned down she sent out a significant donation, some say of a million of rubles, to it and they told me that this is why the main street is called the Millionnaya street. Tver became especially beautiful in the years 1811—1812 when the Grand Duchess Ekaterina Pavlovna, the sister of the later Emperor Aleksandr I who was married to Prince Oldenburg, the Governor-General of Tver, lived in it. The city received significant benefits under the rule of the brother-in-law of the Emperor. A superb palace was built for his family; it was connected by long galleries with two newly built churches, a Russian Orthodox one and a Lutheran one. The palace was built almost next door to the very ancient cathedral…

Dmitry Blagovo

When in Tver you'll want some noodles,
There are two places for good cheese,
Take scrambled eggs or other food,
Mark down Galgnani and Cogloni, please.

        Aleksandr Pushkin

131

At last we arrived at Klin, a town at a distance of 92 versts from Moscow. In Russia inns are located mostly in ordinary village houses, typically rather miserable. A wise traveler prefers to sleep in his carriage.

Martha Wilmot

Near Klin, August 6, 1839. The favorite amusement of the Russian country folk is the swing; this contraption promotes the sense of balance, typical for the inhabitants of this country. One should bear in mind that swinging is a quiet and peaceful occupation—such an amusement is very suitable to the people in which the fear has developed caution. Calm and careful swinging is a kind of a resting period between sessions of zesty powerful swinging. It is an impressive and even frightening sight… When swinging is done in earnest I noticed that no more than two persons, two men or two women, or a man and a woman, are standing on the swing board, each on his own edge, and firmly grasp the ropes on which the swing is suspended to keep their balance. Standing up they swing to a terrible height and at the peak there seems to be a moment coming when the swing will overturn imminently… Russian have supple bodies and surprisingly gracefully and easily keep their balance—the exercise requires outstanding daring as well as adroitness and poise.

Astolphe de Custine

*A curvy dirty lane seems almost as endless
As the great Russian plain itself.
When you have turned into a highway
You've reached the end of dusty journey at the gate…*

Aleksei Apukhtin

134

When I was entering Moscow I was very much impressed with the pillars at the tollhouse, the colored gate barrier, and the military guards and their sparkling bayonets. We have entered the city at last. We are riding along one street after another and do not know where to turn our eyes… How great are the buildings, how grand are the churches, how many people in the streets…

Vasily Selivanov

135

128

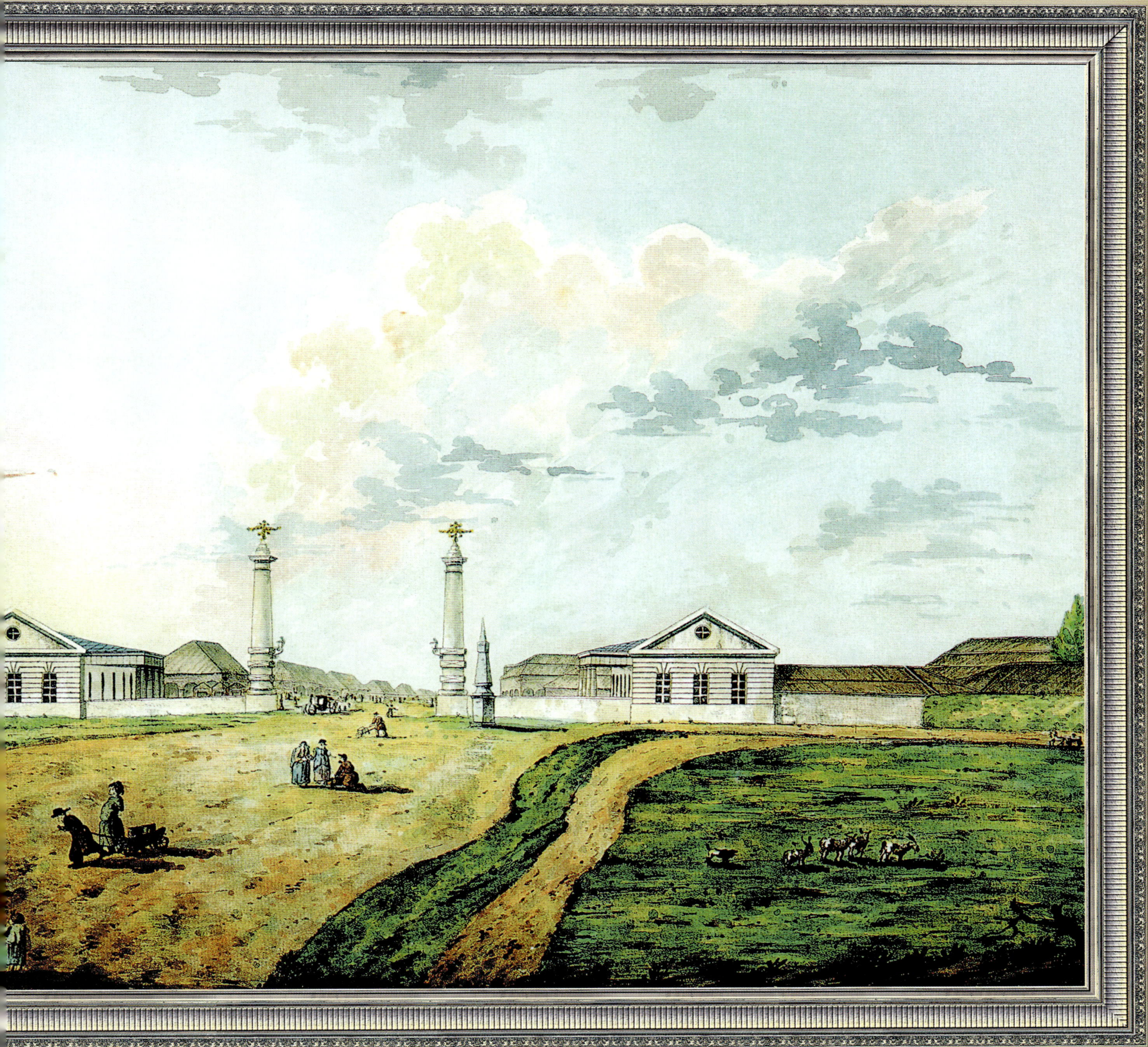

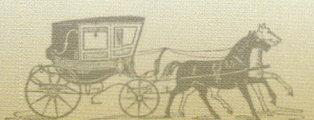

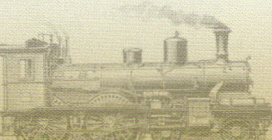

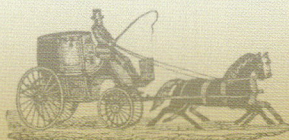

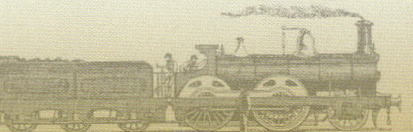

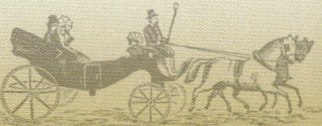

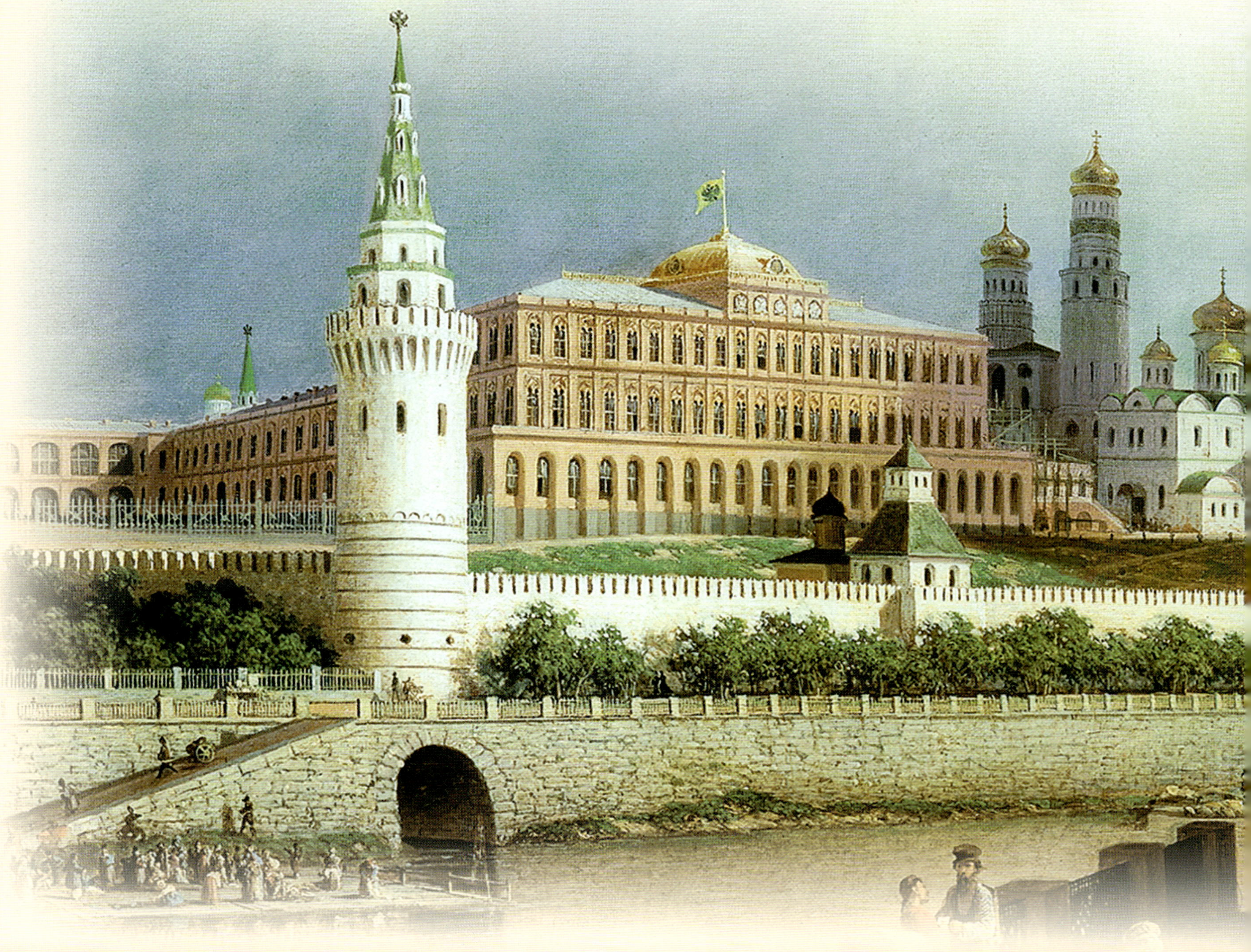

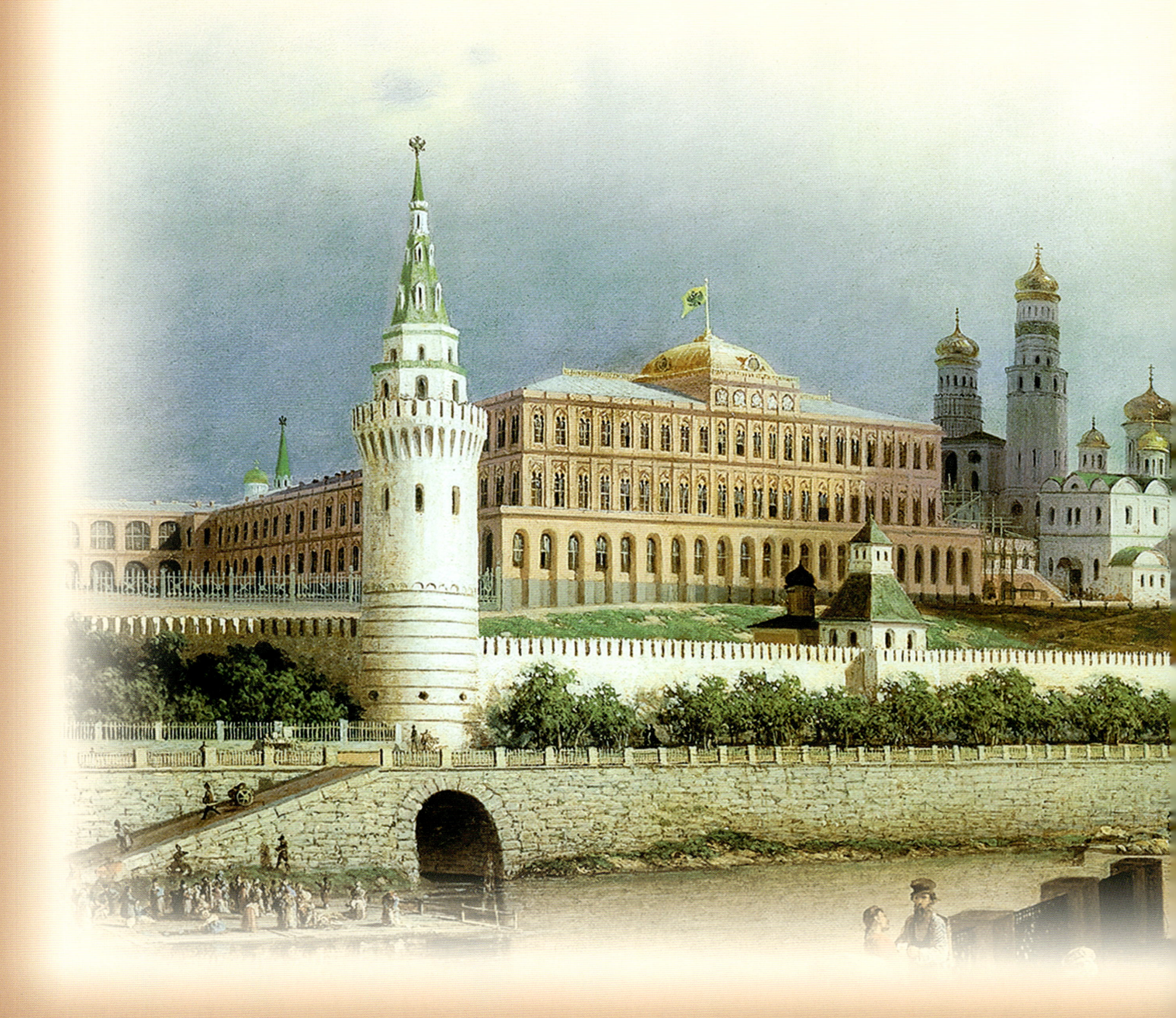

Moscow

Moscow is not just another large city of which there are a thousand, Moscow is not a silent pile of cold stones, by no means it is! It has a soul of its own, it has its life... It has its own language, loud, powerful, divine...

Mikhail Lermontov

Here stands, with shady park surrounded,
Petrovsky Castle; and the fame
In which so lately it abounded
Rings proudly in that somber name.
          Aleksandr Pushkin

We entered our wooden box and started the trip at seven in the evening. Another day full of suffering. We have not seen anything particularly noteworthy until we reached the Petrovsky village from where an astounding view of Moscow is opened. We passed the place where Napoleon stayed when Moscow was on fire. Moscow is a very peculiar city and when you are looking at it seems to be a fairy tale from the Arabian tales of "A Thousand and One Nights".
          Clara Schumann

The Petrovsky Palace is built in the Gothic taste, surrounded with groves of trees and has a peculiar style of its own.
          Gavriyl Gerakov

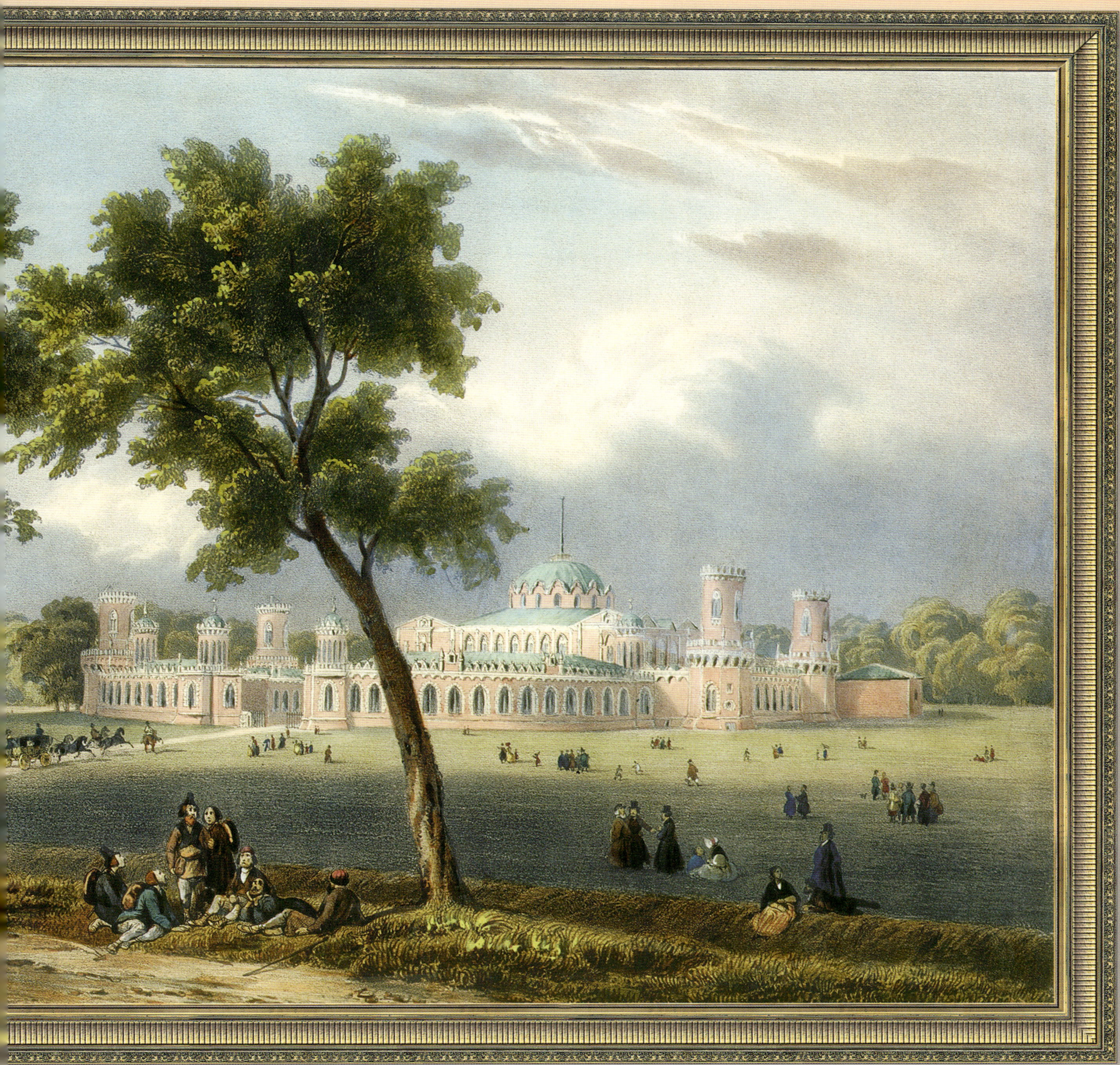

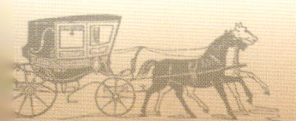

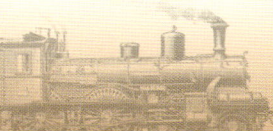

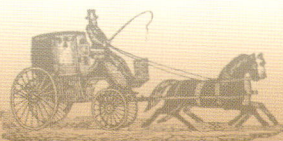

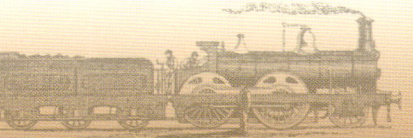

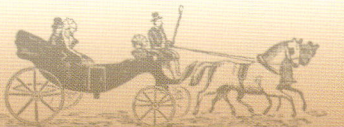

137

*At the very early dawn the sun light
Strikes the church tops shimmering with gold,
Reflections of the mighty walls of royal palace old
Are floating in water crystal-bright.*

Mikhail Lermontov

138

A multitude of church spires, cupolas... and ornate towers were glistening in the sun over clouds of road dust... Try to visualize the sight which is quite impossible to depict by trying to paint it... It is a veritable phantasm that makes Moscow a unique city, one that has no equal in Europe.

Astolphe de Custine

Crowds are jostling, rows of shops are sparkling, street traders are yelling, the constables are busy at the monument commemorating Minin, everything is so lively, so noisy, so hectic! Moscow is not just another big city, one of a thousand. Moscow is not a silent pile of cold stones symmetrically arranged,... no! it has its own soul, its own life.

Mikhail Lermontov

*Friends, how my heart
would leap with pleasure
When suddenly I saw this treasure
Of spires and belfries, in a cup
With parks and mansions, open up.*

Aleksandr Pushkin

Even at a large distance you will glimpse the cupolas of the Moscow churches. Moscow is located in a plain, indeed, the entire Russia is nothing but a vast plain and therefore when you are approaching a large city you can even fail to notice how extensive it is. Somebody noted aptly that Moscow is a village rather than a city. Everything is mixed up there—the humble huts, townhouses, palaces, markets similar to Oriental ones, churches, public institutions, ponds, groves, and parks. In this huge city you will find the entire diversity of the mores and tribes populating Russia... Life is freer here than in Saint-Petersburg where the court inevitable makes its influence felt over everything.

Louise Germaine de Staël

*Already gleaming
Before their eyes they see unfold
The towers of white stone Moscow beaming
With fire from every cross of gold.*

Aleksandr Pushkin

The Kremlin is located at the very center of Moscow on a high hill and can be easily seen from all points. It is surrounded with a serrated wall in the Gothic style; one can enter it through two massive gates or over bridges guarded by soldiers... A magnificent and picturesque view of the river, the huge city and its environs opens from the Kremlin hill. The landscape is made to look even more beautiful by the palaces, the gilded spires of the distant churches, and the extensive never-ending pine and mixed forests.

Martha Wilmot

The rest of the Kremlin is occupied by the palace of the emperors, the Senate building and two very strange temples. All these edifices of magnificent architecture are standing around the military parade square.

Jean Larreil

(144)

*My fancy is to follow the people
Into the church to join the crowd
Under the gold cross to hear prayers loud…*
Aleksandr Polezhaev

The Kremlin accommodates the ancient Tsar's palace and the coronations are still conducted in a small square. The crown, the orb, the tsar's regalia, etc. are stored at a special place.
Martha Wilmot

(145)

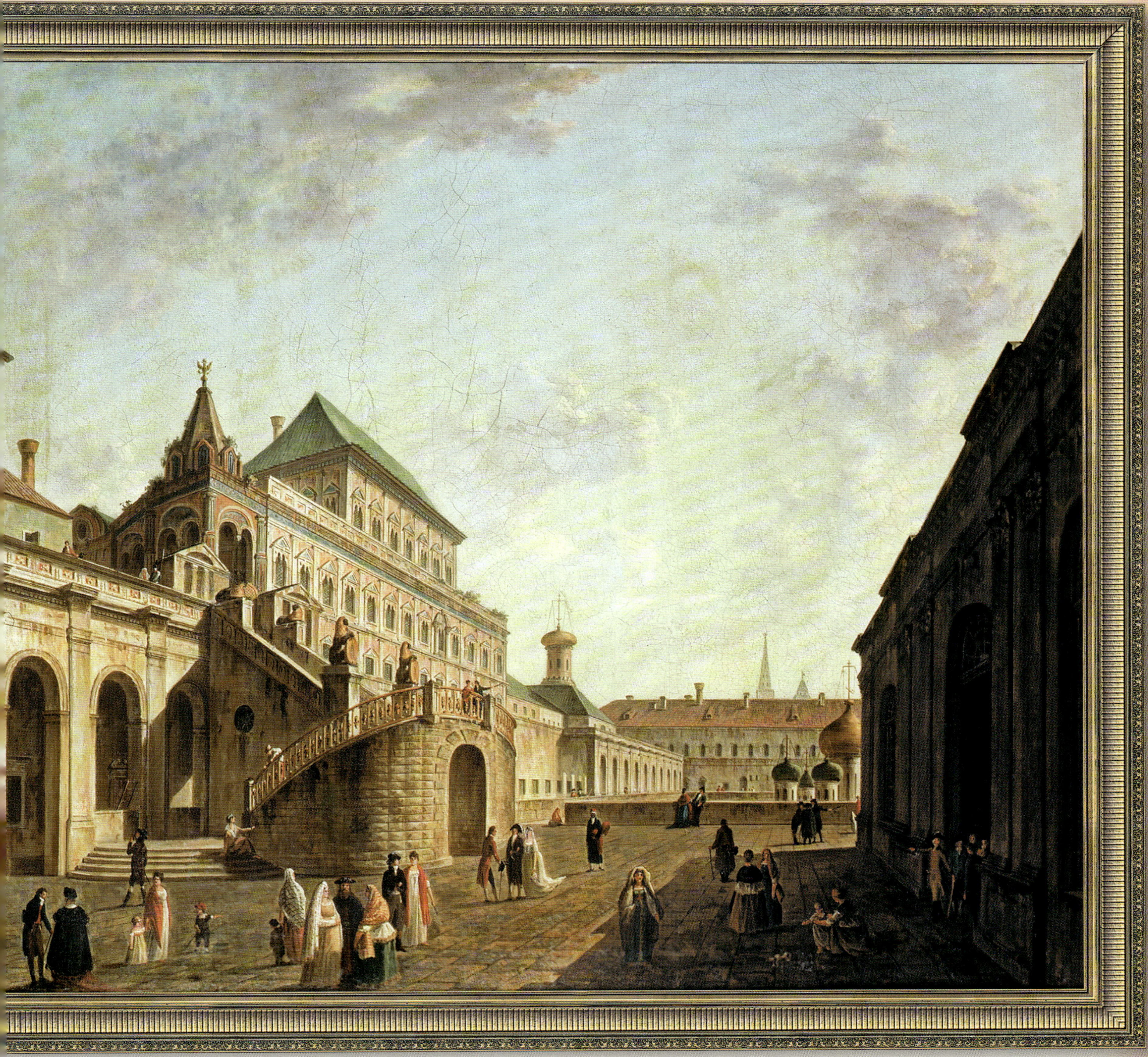

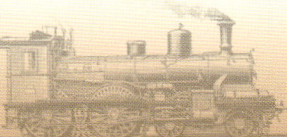

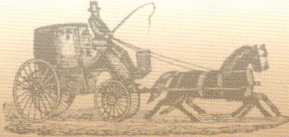

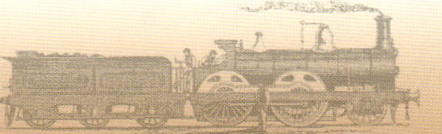

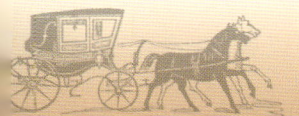

Again it's Moscow I see!
The fog has cleared away
Ivan the Great is looming before me,
Its cross shines brightly gay.

Aleksandr Polezhaev

An almost cylinder-shaped tower known as Ivan the Great bell tower was looming between two churches. It resembled an Egyptian minaret. Many bells of various sizes are hung on the tower and one amazingly large bell, noted by historians, is lying on the ground near the tower. From the top of the tower one can view the entire city which looks like a star with four points split into two which are made especially picturesque by the multicolored house roofs and the silver- and gold-plated tops of numerous churches and belfries.

Jean Larreil

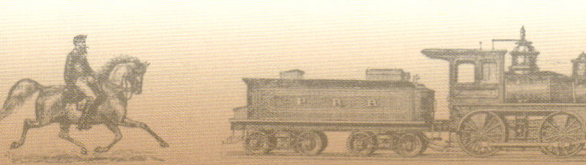

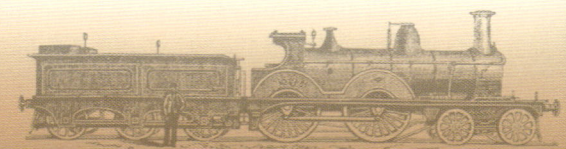

148

144

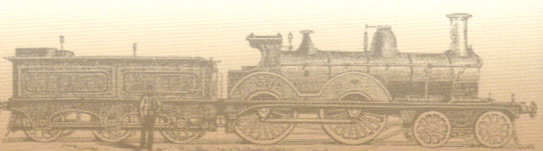

*The light of dawn made Kremlin shine
In magic hues of ruby fine
Above the glorious city mine.*

   Evgeny Baratynsky

What can be compared to the Kremlin that is surrounded with spiked walls and boasts of the gilded cathedral cupolas while lying on a high hill as a crown on the head of a mighty ruler?... No, one just cannot describe either the Kremlin, or its strong walls, or its dark passages, or its luxurious palaces... One just has to see it, to sense everything that they tell to one's heart and imagination.

   Mikhail Lermontov

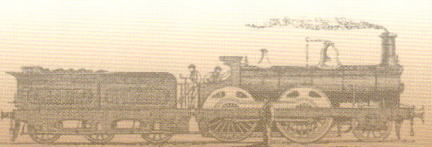

151

*It is encircled with plowed fields,
Its orchards sprouting rich blossom,
In many temples on seven hills
Its numerous belfries are handsome!*

Fedor Glinka

The Kremlin is a fortress that supported the Russian Tsars in their wars against the Tartars; it is surrounded with a tall wall with merlons and towers at the corners; the towers look more like Turkish minarets than fortifications because of their strange shapes. Though the city buildings look Oriental in their appearance one sees the effects of Christianity everywhere. It is witnessed by the numerous churches which are highly respected in Russia and which attract your eye at every step in the city. One tends unwittingly to compare Moscow to Rome but not because there is a similarity between them in the building styles… It is the amazing blend of the rural serenity and the opulent palaces, the vast expanse of the city and the multitude of churches that establish a similarity between the Rome of Asia to the Rome of Europe.

Louise Germaine de Staël

Sons of great nation, you did vanquish foes,
You saved the Russian tsars, your glory unsurpassed!
The best memorial to you is people's awards and honors,
And that the Holy Russia will for ever last!

Nikolai Stankevich

153

The first thing that draws your eye when you enter the Red Square is the Pozharsky and Minin memorial… The sculptured group is beautifully depicting the gallantry of the characters. Lord Pozharsky is presented by the inexplicable fantasy of the sculptor sitting in a classical attire holding a sword in his right hand and placing his left arm on a shield. Minin, a merchant from Nizhni Novgorod, is taking a step towards him, placing his left hand on the sword held by the prince and raising his right arm as if calling for help. The inscription on the pedestal of the monument says "The grateful Russia to the merchant Minin and Prince Pozharsky. Year 1818".

Alexandre Dumas

154

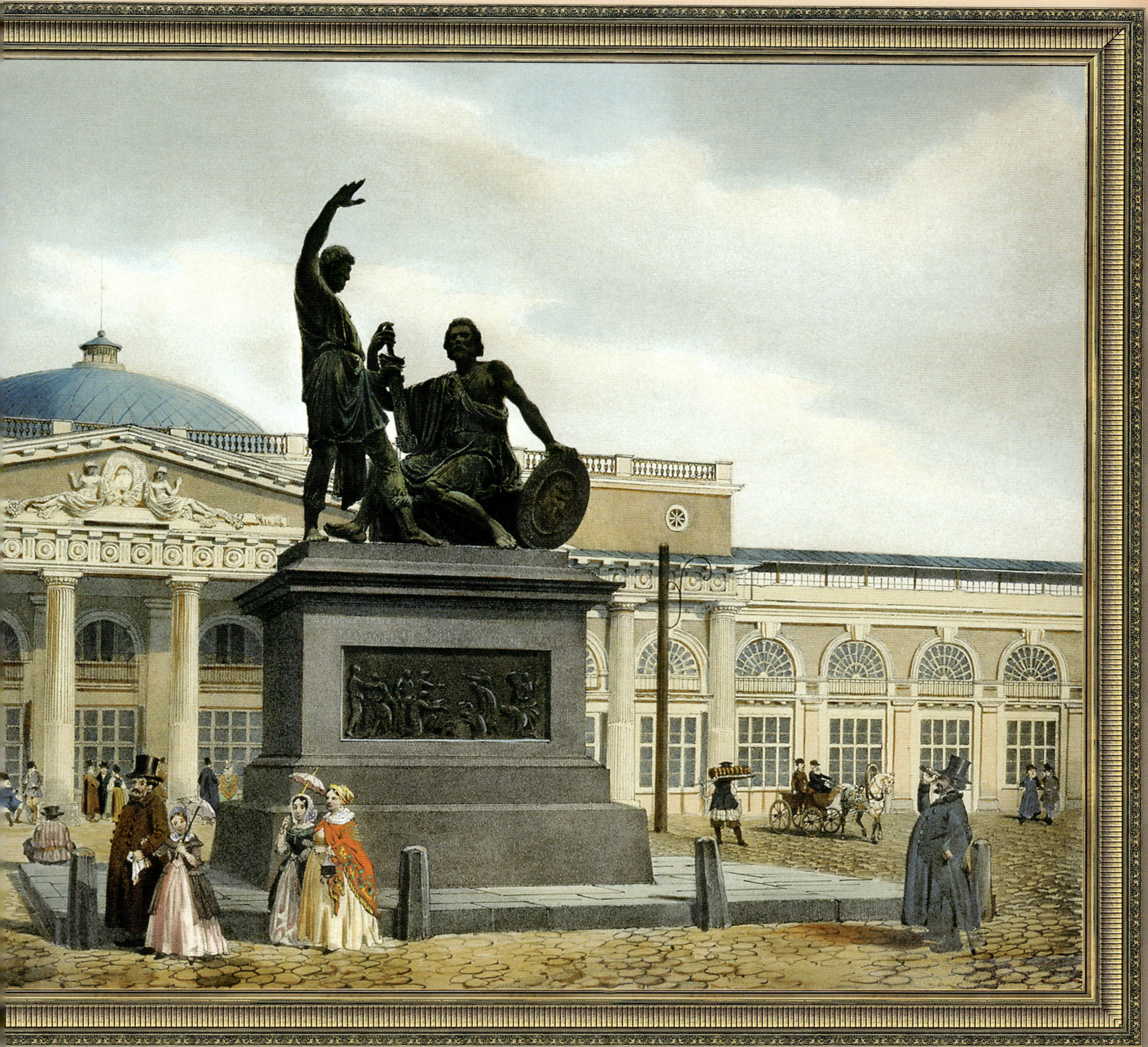

150

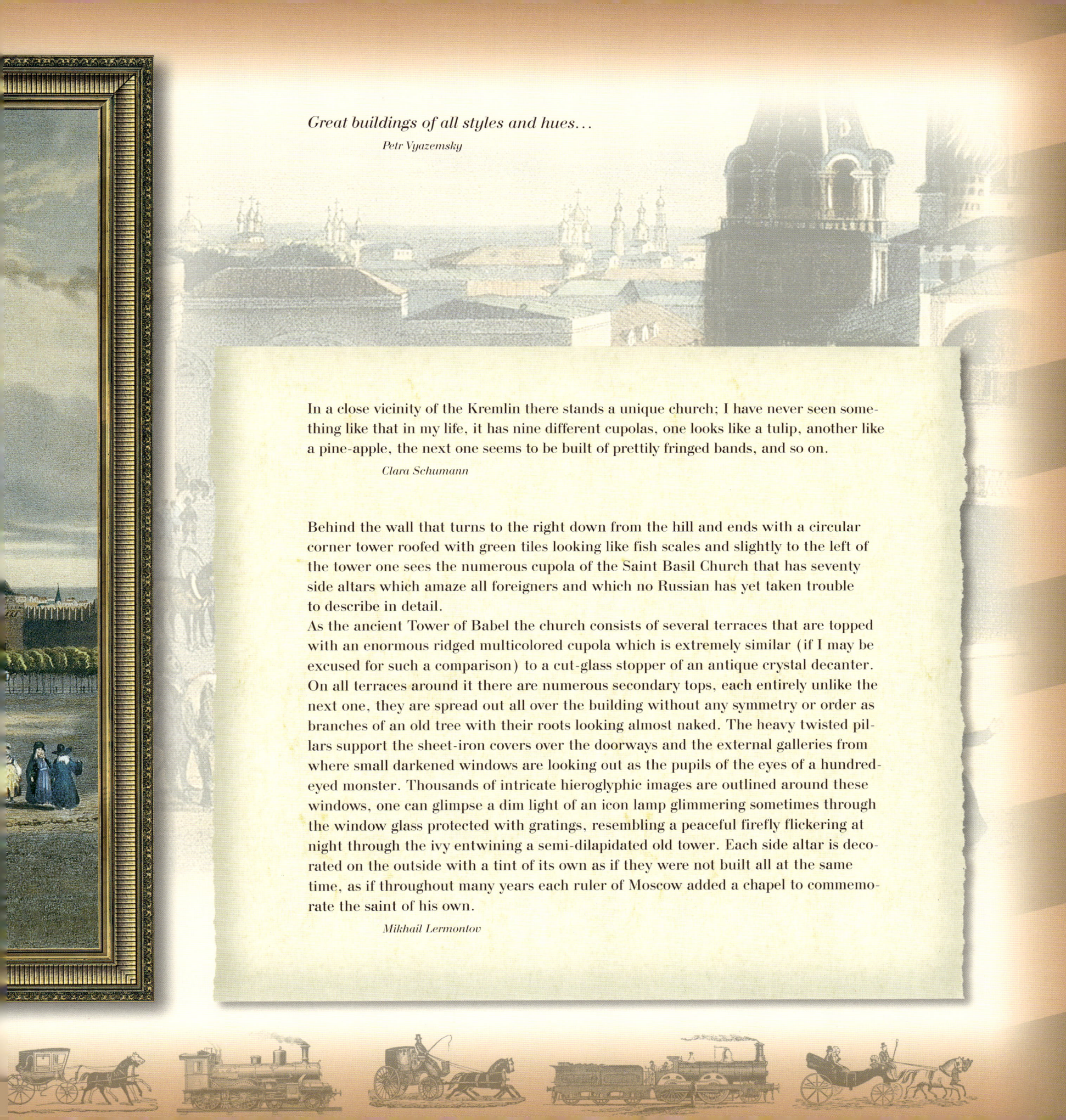

Great buildings of all styles and hues…
  Petr Vyazemsky

In a close vicinity of the Kremlin there stands a unique church; I have never seen something like that in my life, it has nine different cupolas, one looks like a tulip, another like a pine-apple, the next one seems to be built of prettily fringed bands, and so on.
  Clara Schumann

Behind the wall that turns to the right down from the hill and ends with a circular corner tower roofed with green tiles looking like fish scales and slightly to the left of the tower one sees the numerous cupola of the Saint Basil Church that has seventy side altars which amaze all foreigners and which no Russian has yet taken trouble to describe in detail.
As the ancient Tower of Babel the church consists of several terraces that are topped with an enormous ridged multicolored cupola which is extremely similar (if I may be excused for such a comparison) to a cut-glass stopper of an antique crystal decanter. On all terraces around it there are numerous secondary tops, each entirely unlike the next one, they are spread out all over the building without any symmetry or order as branches of an old tree with their roots looking almost naked. The heavy twisted pillars support the sheet-iron covers over the doorways and the external galleries from where small darkened windows are looking out as the pupils of the eyes of a hundred-eyed monster. Thousands of intricate hieroglyphic images are outlined around these windows, one can glimpse a dim light of an icon lamp glimmering sometimes through the window glass protected with gratings, resembling a peaceful firefly flickering at night through the ivy entwining a semi-dilapidated old tower. Each side altar is decorated on the outside with a tint of its own as if they were not built all at the same time, as if throughout many years each ruler of Moscow added a chapel to commemorate the saint of his own.
  Mikhail Lermontov

156

When we left the Pokrovsky Cathedral we went down to the holy gate of the Kremlin; in order to observe the custom rigorously enforced by the Russians, I entered into the gateway, which was rather narrow, however, after taking off my hat. I was told that the custom originated at the time of the last invasion of the Kalmyks when only the miraculous intervention of the heavenly forces stopped the enemy from penetrating the fortress. The saints have been known to fail things but on that day they were on the alert, the Kremlin was left unharmed and intact and the Russians keep on taking off their hats to express their gratitude to their glorious benefactors.

Astolphe de Custine

157

*…Who will dare to keep his hat
At the sacred Kremlin gate?*

Fedor Glinka

*By contrast, in the frozen season,
How pleasantly the stages pass.*
   Aleksandr Pushkin

We have climbed up the bell tower of the Ivan the Great from where the most spectacular and expansive view is opened. The scene is wonderfully enlivened by the river which intersects the city as a silver half-moon. Hundreds of frenzied Arabian, Livonian and Tartar steeds are charging ahead along the ice path marked up by the green branches steered by gentlemen sitting in small shell-shaped *traîneaux*. The brave men slid down from the enormous ice mountains at such a speed that their descent could be compared only to flying. There are numerous holes in a separate section of the ice cover on the river and rows or launder women are bent busily wringing off their laundry despite the bitter frost. Fishermen are hauling onto the ice baskets with fish as large as a rural hut…

   Catherine Wilmot

*A coat of arms is shining on a palace
That bears witness to exalted rank,
A poor cottage next to it is not a menace
Its kitchen garden yields cucumbers lank.*

      Petr Vyazemsky

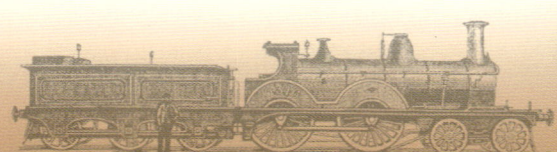

The famous Pashkov palace built in the Italian style is enormous in size and cost millions. Its interior and exterior decorations would make it suitable for serving as a royal residence…

G. Reinbeck

Moscow served as a meeting place for the entire Russian gentry who came from all provinces to spend winter there. The dazzling young guards officers hurried there from Saint-Petersburg. Music was playing throughout the ancient capital, all public places were crowded. Twice a week five thousand people gathered at the ballroom of the Assembly Hall for the gentry. Young people met each other there, romances sprang and weddings were arranged. Moscow was as famous for its nubile young gentlewomen as Vyazma was famous for its cakes.

Aleksandr Pushkin

It is amazing how many solid stone buildings there are and how often they are standing side by side with lanes full of primitive wooden huts. If one could assemble together all the fine magnificent structures some of which are gorgeous and erase the poor huts Moscow would be the most beautiful of the cities.

G. Reinbeck

162

The poetry lives side by side with trade…
Petr Vyazemsky

163

164

The trading institutions of Moscow also exhibit an Asiatic character. The traders in turbans and in various Oriental clothes are displaying to you rare goods: the Siberian furs and Indian fabrics could easily satisfy the luxurious tastes of the Russian nobility whose imagination is equally lit up by the sable fur of northern tribes and by the rubies from Persia.

Louise Germaine de Staël

*They say it's Europe and Asia,
The heritage of Romans, Orient, and Slav,
We sense an inkling of primordial leisure
In everything before our eyes we have.*

   Petr Vyazemsky

165

166

There are thousands of small things that make Moscow look like an Asiatic city! Below the crosses the church spires carry glittering crescents which symbolize the triumph of the Christianity and they are shining as brightly as the gilt church domes. Within a radius of twenty six miles from the Kremlin there are private and public parks and gardens, fine bell towers, theaters, arches, hospitals and monasteries, and the vast palaces guarded by growling monster beasts and surrounded with walls. Giant figures of the saints are painted in radiant gold colors on the church walls and thousands of people are crossing themselves and lie face down on the ground before them.

   Catherine Wilmot

The Moscow merchants and women wear fascinating clothes: men have long coats belted at the waistline and women tie silk kerchiefs over their heads. They never wear hats. The rural women looked especially striking (it was the Easter week when the country people flock over to the city for entertainment) in the silk Kazan jackets fringed with fur over, for instance, a simple print cotton dress.

   Clara Schumann

167

168

In the wide square there looms the Petrovsky theater, a product of the newest art, a great building constructed according to the best taste with a flat roof and an imposing portico on top of which there immovably stands the alabaster Apollo on one leg in his alabaster chariot drawn by three alabaster horses who is looking with annoyance at the Kremlin walls which jealously protect the ancient relics of Russia from him.

Mikhail Lermontov

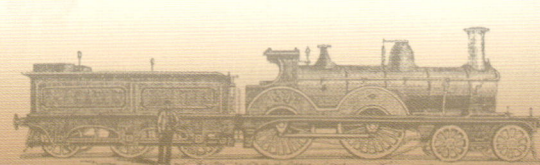

The house is packed out; scintillating,
The boxes; boiling, pit and stalls;
The gallery claps—it's bored with waiting
And up the rustling curtain crawls.

Aleksandr Pushkin

I was amazed and delighted by the grand Petrovsky theater that had arisen from the old burned-out ruins that had been an eyesore for the residents of Moscow for more than twenty years. I was greatly impressed with everything I saw—the splendid theater auditorium which is one of the largest in Europe, full of spectators, the gorgeous garments of the ladies, the bright lights, the excellent scenery, and the richly staged performances.

Sergei Aksakov

170

The palaces surrounded with gardens look more like the country castles than the city dwellings and these luxurious edifices are bordered with rows of carefully painted wooden huts, churches, monasteries, parks, and then fields, pastures, and lakes... The people enliven the city scenes and make them seem even more attractive for a foreigner.

Leon de Bussier

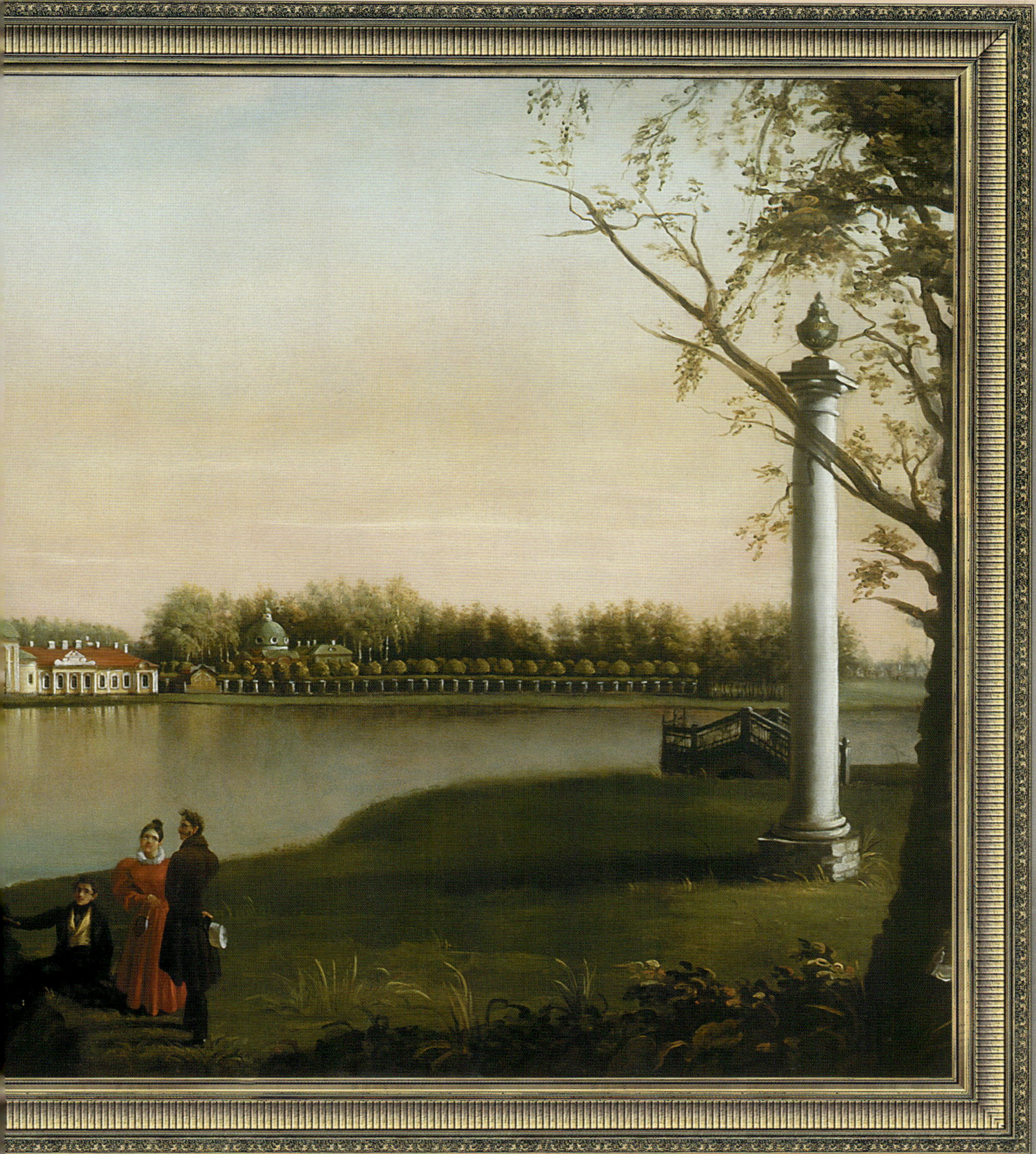

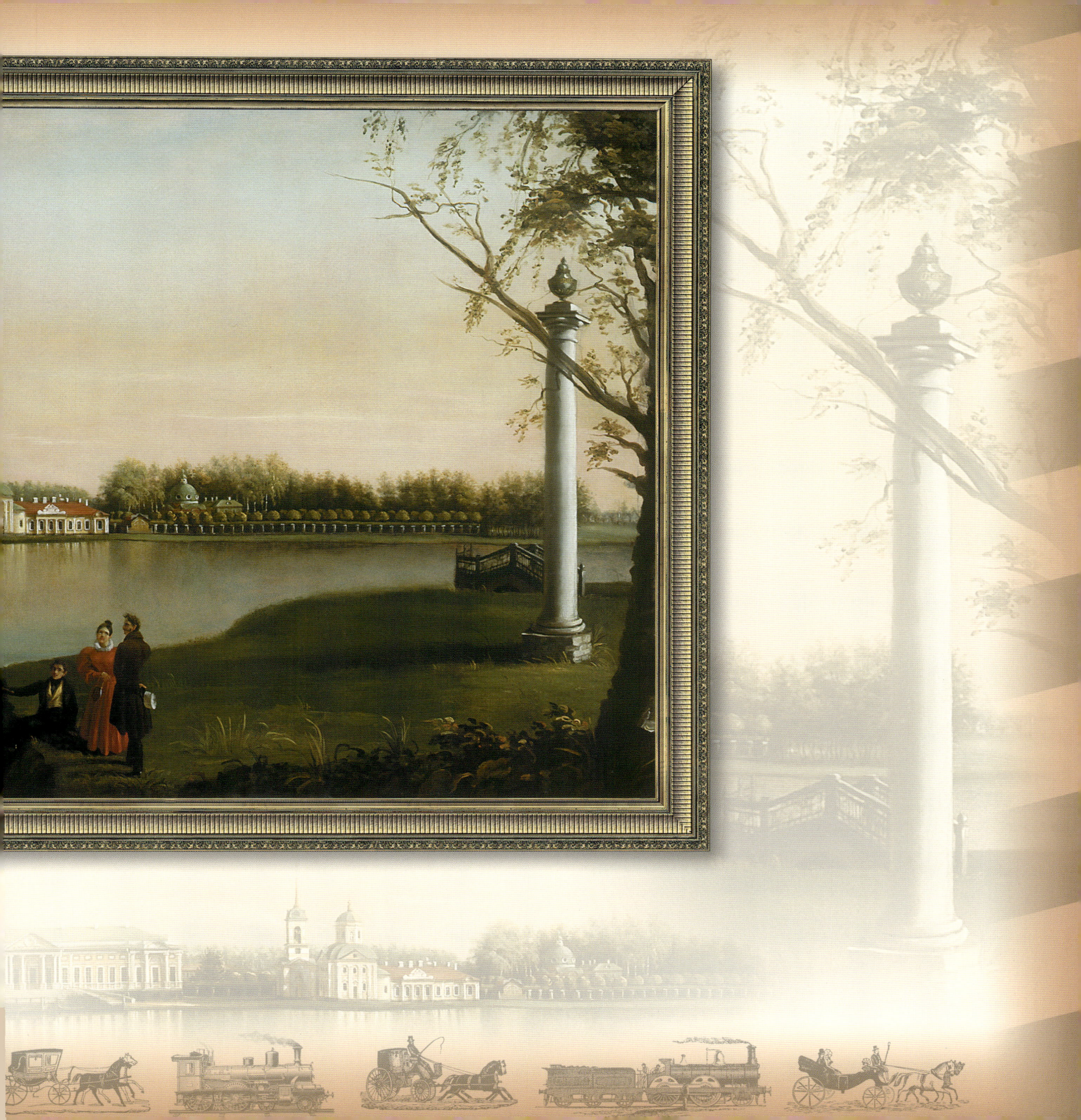

*The people in the streets are rushing
The coaches dash, the carriages buzz,
The bells are eternally tolling.*

Vladimir Filimonov

171

Moscow differs from Saint-Petersburg in that the streets are not so regular and there are no such huge and poorly proportioned buildings. The streets are not very wide, arranged without any symmetry, and very picturesque because of the uneven terrain. The city is ringed with a green belt of many wide boulevards overgrown with beautiful trees and flowers. The buildings are arranged in disorder, the church cupolas and the belfry spires are looming over their flat roofs that seem piled one over another.

Leon de Bussier

Here is a glorious spot for leisure time. The central wide road is planted with lime trees on the sides… Splendid flower beds are planted at the sides, there are two pools with water… in summer time fountain pipes are inserted in the evenings and the water is squirted to the height of ten feet or more. Many people are gathering there daily for recreation.

"Moscow, historical guide"

172

173

*And now we see a-shimmer
The pillars of the turnpike-gate;
Along Tverskaya Street already
The potholes make the coach unsteady.*

Aleksandr Pushkin

When a resident of Saint-Petersburg enters Moscow for the first time he sees a world that is novel for him. He will be shown the Tverskaya Street and he will be amazed to see that a house has moved ahead a few steps into the street as if to see what is going on in the street while another house has moved back as it is too conceited or too shy depending on its appearance; that a dilapidated wooden hut has fitted snugly and modestly between two rather large stone houses; that a tiny tobacco shop, or a dirty tavern, or a similarly dirty inn leans to a splendid fashionable dress shop. Our Saint-Petersburg resident will be even more amazed to feel that the queer weirdness of the street possesses a beauty of its own.

Vissarion Belinsky

168

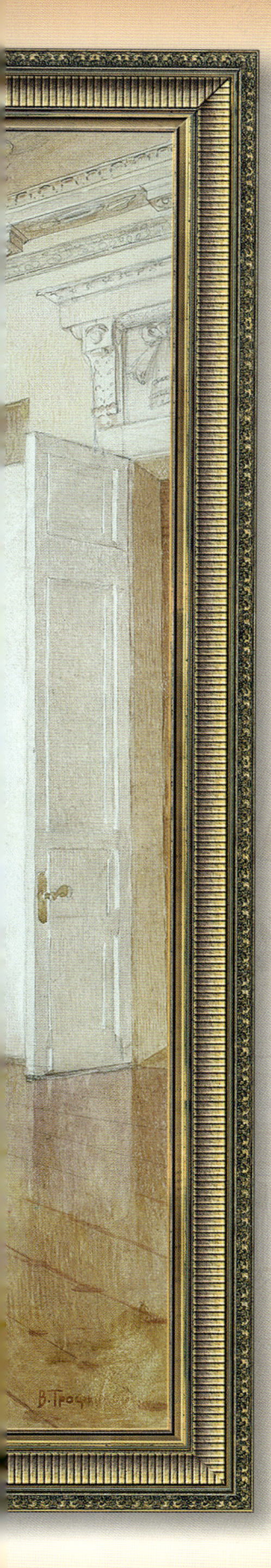

The fine four-storey house is one of the largest buildings in the entire Tverskaya Street. This is the house of General Field Marshal Zakhar Chernyshev. It was bought by the government in 1784 to serve as the residence of the Moscow governor-general. It attracts attention because of its superior architecture, all parts of it look magnificent, at the main entrance there stand giant figures depicting allegorical mythological deities executed by a good sculptor.. Before the mansion of the governor-general there is a rather large square-shaped public area…

"Moscow, historical guide"

The magnificent exterior of the mansion agreed with the luxurious interior decorations. Expensive wood paneling of all types, marble, cut glass, bronze, silver, and gold were employed for embellishing the rooms where the mirror ceilings reflected the brilliantly lit chandeliers while the multi-colored hardwood parquet floors resembled exquisite carpeting.

Mikhail Pylyaev

…We visited also a Russian tavern where we saw the common people behaving in their distinctive truly Russian fashion. Cab drivers, artisans, and other working people came there to drink tea.

Clara Schumann

A Muscovite's face never seems worried, it always looks kind-hearted and he candidly looks at you as if intending to ask you: where are you lunching today?

Vissarion Belinsky

Inns and taverns are all over the city but the best are concentrated near the government offices, the Kremlin garden, and along the Il'inka Street.

Petr Wistenhof

*Oh, Moscow! Please, keep your native virtue
Under your flashy dress!*

Petr Vyazemsky

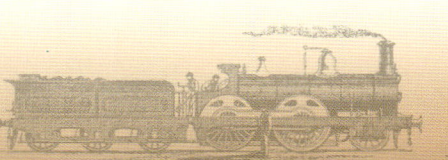

*Then our Automedons are flashing,
Our troikas effortlessly dashing.*

Aleksandr Pushkin

181

Moscow is famous for the elegance of the carriages but they are not distinguished by their strength. The *droshky* carriages are especially fine, very elegant with curved extremely elastic suspension trusses; one can ride softly in them as if in a rocking cradle while freely seeing everything around. In Saint-Petersburg luxurious carriages are often drawn by poor horses while here the most beautiful horses pull old-fashioned carriages.

Johann von Ungern-Sternberg

182

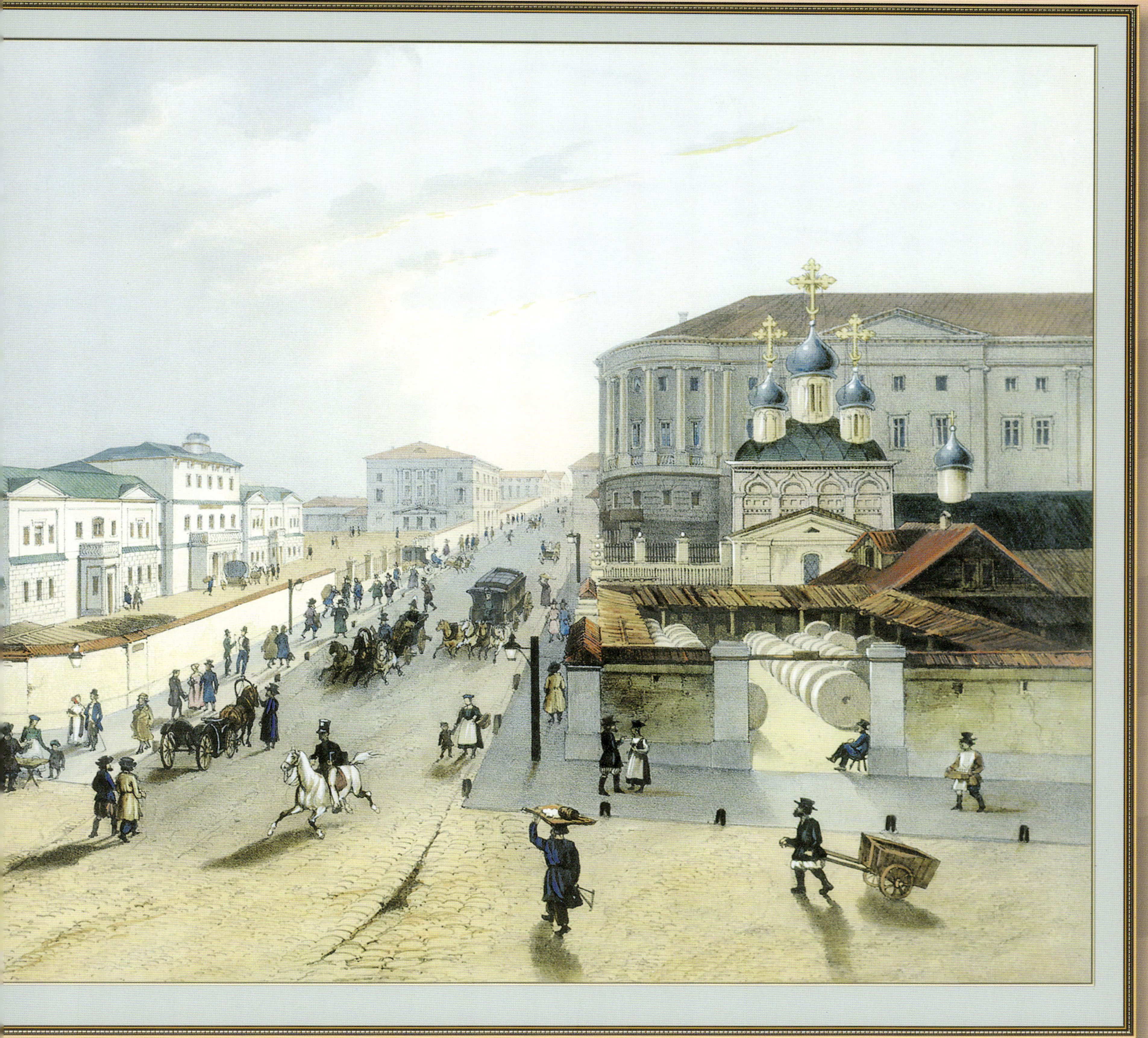

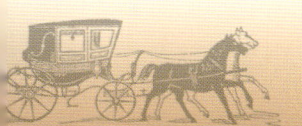

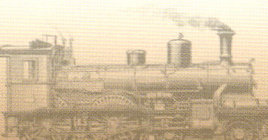

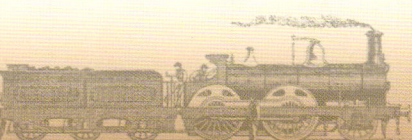

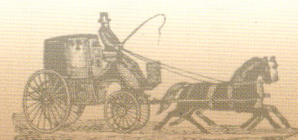

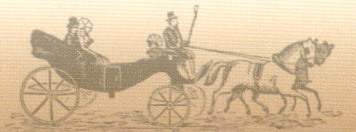

*I greet you, the Devichy Field
Where the holy convent stands.*

　　　　Aleksandr Polezhaev

183

According to a legend, the Devichy Field was given the name of the Devichy (Maiden's) field because rural maidens were taking cows to graze grass there. An older legend tells us that at the time of the Tartar rule over Russia Muscovites brought girl slaves to surrender to Tartars to this field. The huge buildings of the Novodevichy Convent are in the Devichy Field…

　　　　Mikhail Pylyaev

184

174

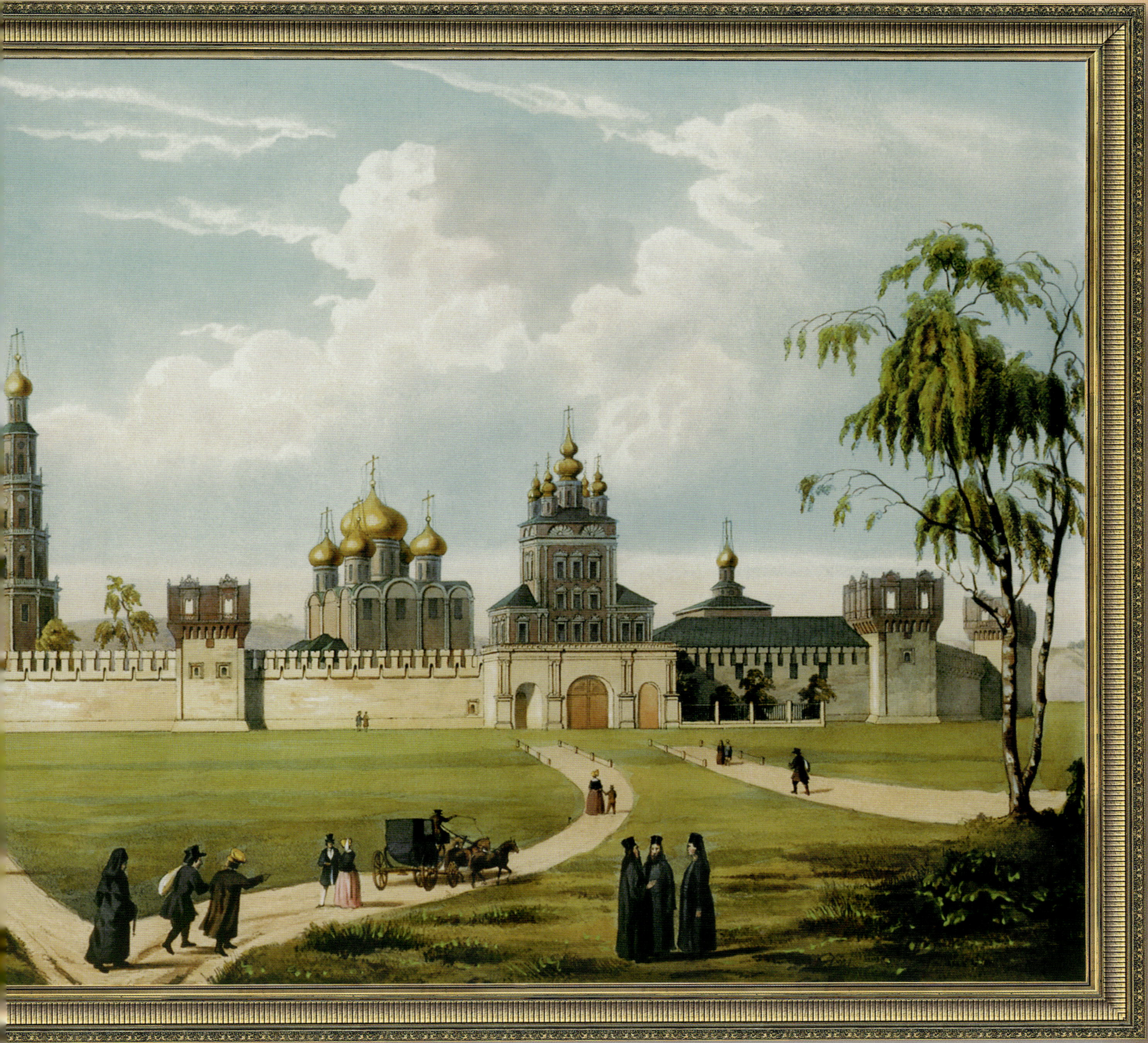

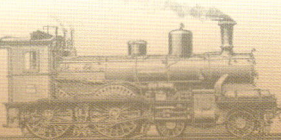

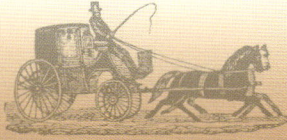

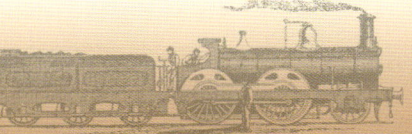

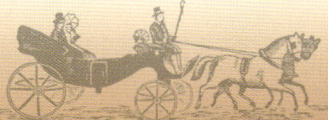

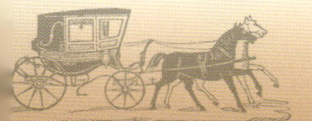

Along the quiet banks of Moskva river
The ancient domed churches stand,
The crosses on their cupolas are leaning,
The shady woods are drawing near
To hills, the convent walls are looming,
Tall and grand…

        Aleksandr Pushkin

We have arisen very early in the morning in order to go to the Vorobievy Hills from where one can see an excellent panorama of Moscow. The seven hundreds of churches and monasteries of various architectural styles, all with gilded cupolas and spires, tall trees in the city parks, the hills on which Moscow is built and, finally, the Kremlin ringed with a wall at the very center of the city—everything makes an extremely strong impression while I was simply charmed with the view… A wide plain at the foot of the Vorobievy Hills makes the view even more magnificent. The plain is bordered by the river which I thought was circling Moscow. However, the river flows throughout the city itself and even reaches under the Kremlin walls.

        Martha Wilmot

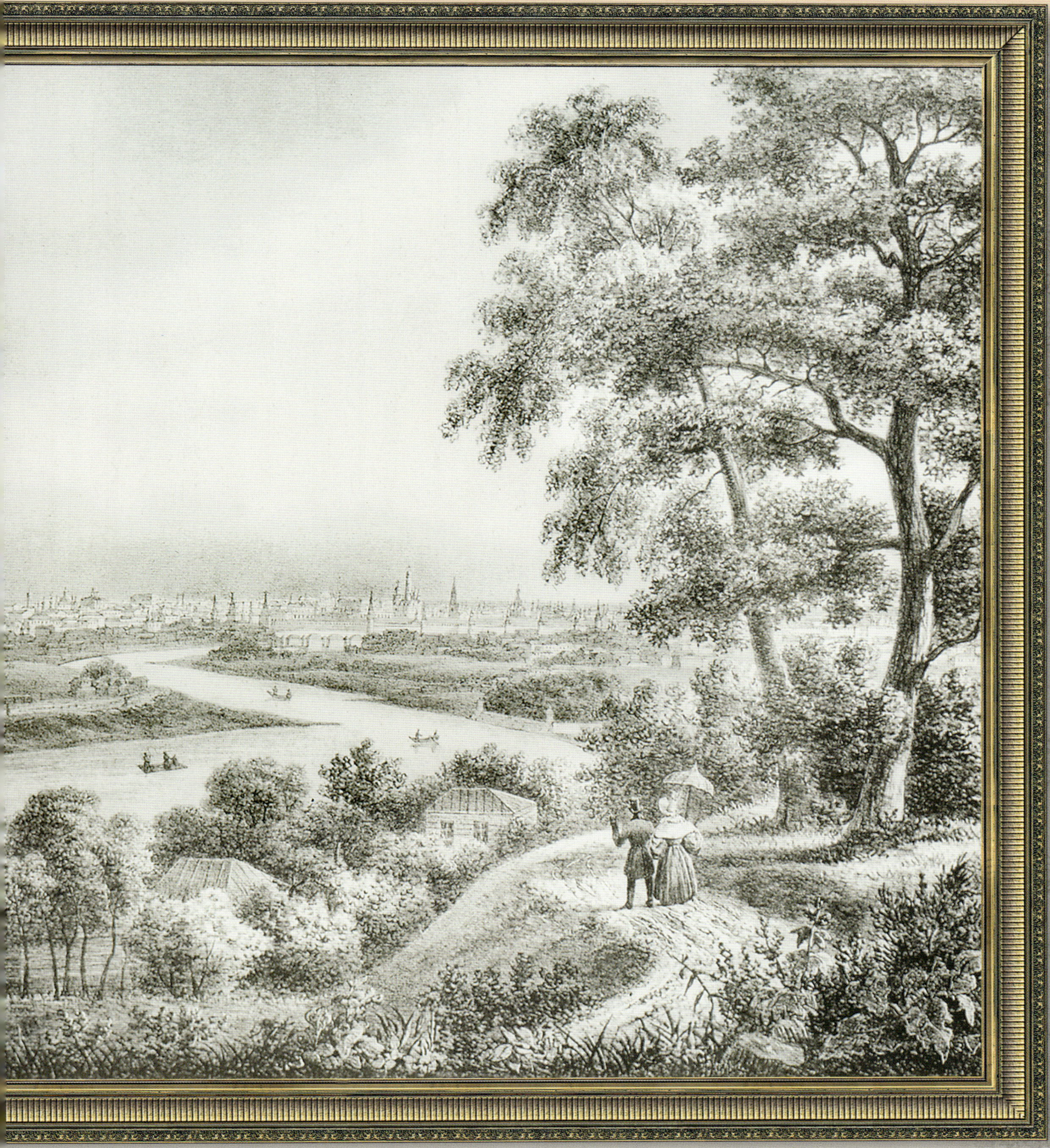

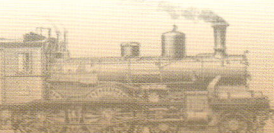

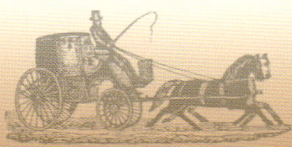

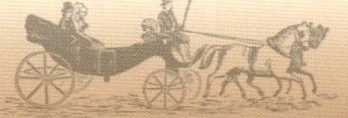

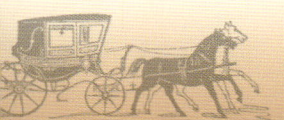

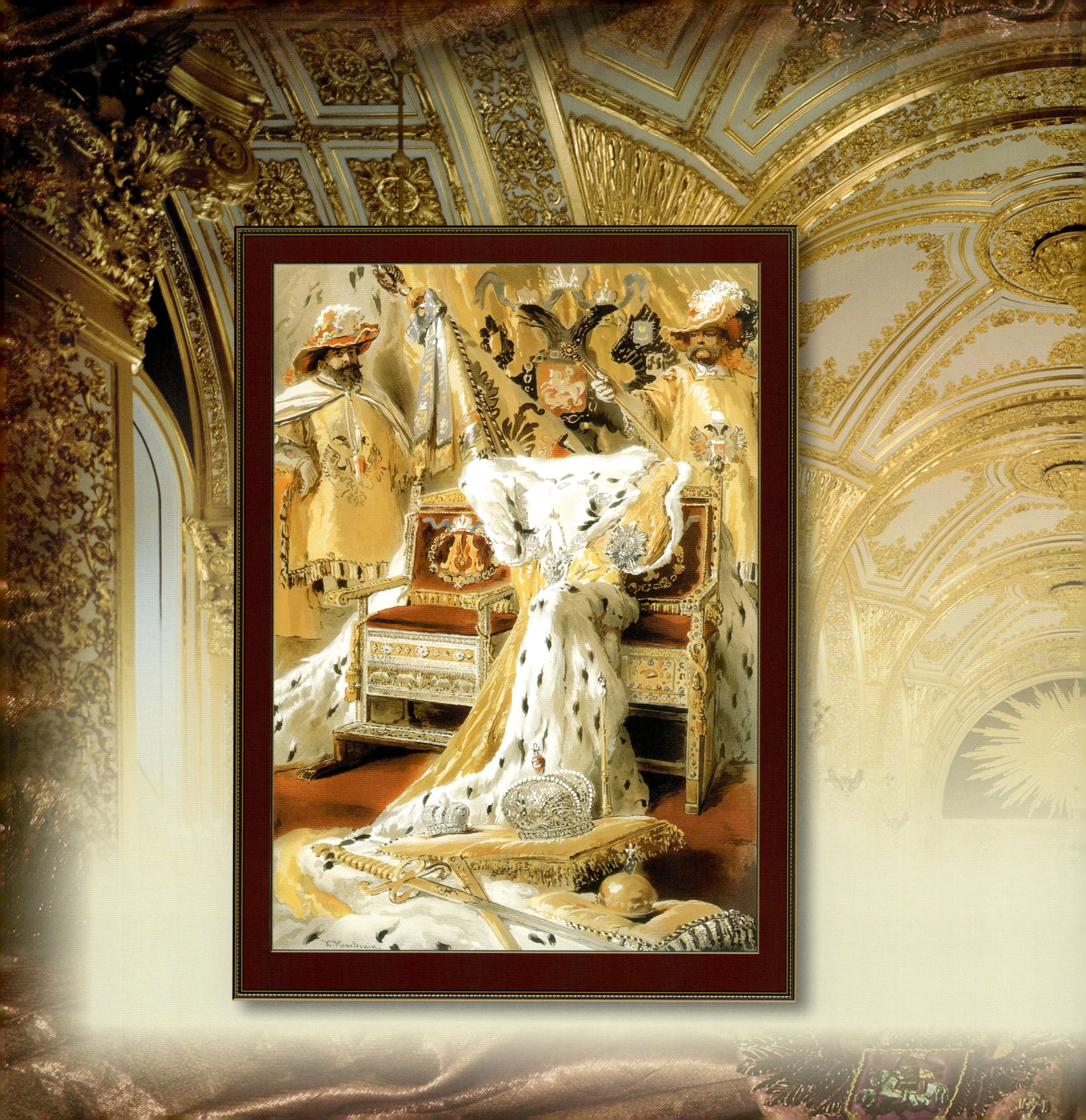

Coronation festivities

The magnificence of the scene in the Cathedral was producing an overwhelming indescribable impression… It was the extraordinary beauty and splendor, the saintly singing, and the prayerful atmosphere going straight into one's heart—everything fused harmoniously uplifting one's soul and flooding it with rapture…

Grand Duke Konstantin Konstantinovich

Saint-Petersburg was officially founded as the capital city of the Russian Empire in 1713. The tsar issued stern instructions ordering all governmental institutions to be transferred from Moscow to the new capital and prohibiting new construction in Moscow. The rich landed gentry, the noblemen serving in the government and armed forces as well as the rare artists and scholars started leaving Moscow for Saint-Petersburg. As the great Russian poet Pushkin said, "The old Moscow had to bend its head before its younger rival, as a queen dowager before a newly crowned queen".

Peter the Great regarded the ancient capital of Russia as a symbolic representation of backwardness, the medieval savagery, and the fierce resistance to his reforms. Peter's successors in late 18th century no longer had such harsh feelings about Moscow. Catherine the Great promulgated the "Proclamation of Liberties and Freedoms for All Russian Nobility" in 1762 and granted the celebrated "Charter of Rights and Freedoms and Privileges of the Nobility" in 1785 releasing the landed gentry from the obligation to take military or government service. By that action the gentry were allowed to lead private lives wherever they wished and the society life in Moscow became much livelier in consequence.

Even though Catherine the Great scorned Moscow as a "republic of the gentry" she was aware of the significant contribution made by the historical roots to strengthening of the Imperial power. The Empress established such large charitable institutions in Moscow as The Orphanage, the Golitsyn Hospital, and the Izmailovo Almshouse. M.M. Medoks opened the Petrovsky Theater to the public, new colossal Imperial palaces and impressive public buildings were erected, luxurious private mansions were built in the city and its environs, and a comprehensive program of public works and refurbishment was launched in Moscow.

The invasion of the French army in 1812 was of an especial significance as it enhanced the public awareness of the historic role played by Moscow for the Russian nation. A 19th-century Russian publicist Aleksandr Herzen pointed out: "Peter the Great demoted Moscow from the status of the Imperial capital but Emperor Napoleon (willingly but unwittingly) raised it to the status of the capital of the Russian people. The people was hurt by the news that the enemy had captured Moscow and became conscious of its vital loyalty to it. A new era began for Moscow from that point."

The status of Moscow as the national heart of Russia was ultimately shaped in the aftermath of the Patriotic War of 1812 while the historic landmarks of Moscow were recognized as symbols of national heritage and acquired major public eminence.

However, even in the 18th century when Moscow was obviously subordinate to Saint-Petersburg both in the governmental affairs and in public life it was still regarded as the Elder capital city of Russia. Accordingly, in all official documents Moscow was referred to as the "Sovereign City of Moscow". It was at the Uspensky Cathedral in the Moscow Kremlin that thee conducted the ceremony of the enthronement of the Russian Emperors that served as a symbol of the investment of the right to the autocratic rule to the new monarch.

Peter the Great paid a particular personal attention to the formulation of the enthronement ceremony for the Russian monarchs. He had proclaimed himself the Emperor, then in the Declaration of November 15, 1723 he announced his intention to crown his spouse Ekaterina Alekseevna and thus he recognized the need for changing the established religious ceremony of crowning the Russian Tsar and creating a magnificent official ritual that would be more suitable to the exalted Imperial rank. Many features of the ceremony were borrowed from the rites traditionally conducted at the West European courts.

The main aspects of the coronation ceremony were worked out by Peter himself who took especial care to imbue it with an extraordinary atmosphere of a grand state function. As the Russian Emperor was invested with the highest authority both in the state and in the Russian Orthodox Church during the coronation he placed the crown on his head with his own hands taking it from the senior member of the Church Synod, typically, the Metropolitan of Novgorod and Saint-Petersburg.

Peter retained the primary components of the ancient coronation ritual which were reading out by the monarch of the Creed of the Russian Orthodox Church and performing sacred rites of anointment and Holy Communion at the altar of the Uspensky Cathedral. The main modification he introduced was to make the ceremony a public function involving many participants. The formal coronation procedure was further adapted for each subsequent coronation to make it look even more distinguished and solemn but its principal elements remained unchanged until the coronation of the last Russian Emperor in 1896. The main steps of the traditional coronation process were the ceremonial arrival to Moscow, formal recitation of the Proclamation on the coronation time in the streets and public spaces of Moscow, the ceremony of transfer of the Crown jewels and Imperial regalia, the ritual procession to the Uspensky Cathedral and back to the Palace, the formal dinner at the Faceted Chamber in the Kremlin, the reception for the foreign envoys, and the public festivities with obligatory free treats laid out in the Moscow thoroughfares for the people. Starting from Peter's time special arrangements were made at the Uspensky Cathedral where a canopy was installed; it was decorated with the Imperial coat-of-arms and the insignia of the ancient Russian princedoms and principalities. The Emperor's throne was mounted and a table for the Imperial regalia was placed under the canopy and special galleries were erected along the cathedral walls with seats for the guests.

The Grand Duke Aleksandr Mikhailovich was profoundly impressed with the coronation of Emperor Aleksandr III at which he was present. Here is his narrative. "The ancient capital city of the Russian tsars met face-to-face the new Russia boasting of unlimited resources and potential. The population of Moscow was almost tripled from late April as hundreds of thousands of visitors and sightseers were flocking in from the Russian provinces and from foreign countries. Special trains arrived at Moscow almost each hour bringing in European monarchs, members of the foreign royal families, and representatives of foreign governments. The Minister of the Imperial Court who was responsible for receiving foreign dignitaries could hardly manage to get to the next railway station on time to oversee the preparations and to ensure the rigorous observance of the reception ceremonies. The coronation festivities started with the pageant celebrating the arrival of the Sovereign and his family to Moscow. The grand dukes and foreign princes riding horses gathered at the entrance of the Troitsky Palace at half to nine to accompany Aleksandr III on his ceremonial entry to the Kremlin. At ten o'clock sharp the Emperor went out of the palace, mounted his steed and gave an order to leave. He was riding alone in front of the procession followed by us; a squadron of guardsmen on horseback rode ahead to announce the imminent arrival of the Imperial convoy to the cheering crowds and the troops lined up along the entire route. A long line of ornate guilt carriages followed the riders. The Empress Maria Fedorovna was in the first carriage.

The crowds and troops continuously cheered the procession as it progressed to the Iverskaya Chapel where the Emperor dismounted and entered the chapel to pay homage to the Icon of Our Lady of Iverskaya. We rode into the Kremlin through the Spassky Gate and approached the Arkhangelsky Cathedral. The initial part of the ceremony ended with the church service conducted by the Metropolitan of Moscow in which the Capella church choir of the Imperial Court was singing. The celebrations on May 15 started with the salvo of 101 guns firing from the Kremlin walls. We were gathered in the Grand Palace hall.

According to the ceremonial ritual, the Emperor and the Empress came out on the Red Porch and thrice deeply bowed to the crowd of many thousands who waited to greet them in the Kremlin. The crowd greeted the Royal family with a thunderous "hooray". That was the pinnacle of the coronation ceremony which prompted us to recall the great Russian tsars of old—starting from Ivan III all the Russian tsars demonstrated their commitment to serve the people by thrice bowing low to them from the steps of the Red Porch. Then the procession moved on to the specially erected platform carpeted with red broadcloth which led to the Uspensky Cathedral.

The royal procession route was lined with rows of the palace guards in 1812 uniforms and high bear-fur hats. The heavy bell on the top of the Ivan the Great bell tower struck a chord and immediately all the bells of the innumerable Moscow churches started ringing solemnly. The glorious sounds of the national anthem sung by a five-hundred-strong choir joined the bell ringing. Looking from above into the sea of human joy I saw faces wet with tears of pride and joy... The Royal couple were met at the cathedral door by three Metropolitans and numerous Archbishops and Bishops who ushered them to the thrones placed at the center...

When the grand moment arrived at last the Metropolitan took the Imperial crown from a red velvet pillow and handed it over to the Tsar. Emperor Aleksandr III placed the crown on his head with his own hands, then took the second crown, turned to the Empress who was kneeling before him and placed the crown on her head. This ritual symbolized the difference between the rights of the Emperor given to him from the divine authority and the prerogatives of the Empress that are passed on her by the Emperor.

The Empress had risen from her knees and then the Royal couple turned to face us sitting in our seats dazzled with the blend of resolute vigor and gracious beauty.

Then the Emperor came up to the iconostasis for the Holy Communion. Since the Russian Monarch is the statutory Head of the Russian Orthodox Church he takes the sacred cup from the hands of the Metropolitan and administers the Holy Communion himself on the coronation day. Then the Empress took the sacrament and the coronation ceremony came to the end. The procession returned to the palace in the same order, the bells again were ringing, the cannons roared, and the crowds cheered even louder when they saw the newly crowned Emperor and Empress. Having arrived to the Red Porch the Emperor and the Empress once again bowed deeply to the crowd and then proceeded to the most ancient room of the palace, the so-called Faceted Chamber, where the Imperial family were served the ceremonial dinner."

The preparations for the coronation festivities resulted in inevitable alterations in the appearance of old Moscow owing to the presence of the Imperial Court and the Imperial guards regiments, erection of the spectator galleries and triumphal arches along the procession route, and each coronation ceremony was accompanied with increasingly lavish fireworks displays and magnificent and intricate street lights arrangements.

The coronation of the Empress Anna Ioannovna was the first after which the official coronation picture book was published. It should be noted that the European custom was in line with the old Russian tradition of preparing illuminated manuscripts describing the enthronement event performed in strict accordance with the ancient ritual. The best-known tome of that type is the "Book of Election and Investiture to Tsardom of the Tsar Mikhail Fedorovich". It was created in 1670s by the craftsmen of the Armoury Chamber at the Kremlin and included numerous illustrations depicting the major events in the life of the first tsar of the Romanov Dynasty. Its content and design undoubtedly had a significant influence on the coronation picture books of the 18th and 19th centuries.

The first coronation picture book in Russia was printed at the printing workshop of the Senate in Moscow in 1730. A year later a German-language version was published in Saint-Petersburg. The engravings in the book depicting the Imperial regalia and the highlights of the coronation ceremony were executed primarily by the artist Ottomar Elliger at the Engraving Shop of the Academy of Sciences. The book commemorating the coronation of Anna Ioannovna included only 19 engravings in comparison to 49 engravings in the book commemorating the coronation of Elizaveta Petrovna. The best artists and architects of Moscow and Saint-Petersburg worked for more than two years on the illustrations for the latter book. The original drawings for the engravings were executed by a "draughtsman team" headed by the Moscow architect Ivan Michurin (he supervised preparations for the coronation festivities in Moscow) and by the Academy artists I.E. Grimmel and I.Ya. Schumacher. All the staff of the Engraving Shop was working on the engravings under supervision of the most prominent Russian engravers of mid-18th century I.A. Sokolov and G.A. Kachalov. The engraving quality was so high that the Academy of Arts reserved copies of the book to be used for training art students. In addition to the architectural drawings of the Triumphal arches, the diagrams of the Uspensky Cathedral and the Imperial palaces, and the pictures depicting the Imperial regalia, various ceremonial utensils and figures, fireworks and lighting arrangements, a fairly large numbers of the illustrations represented interiors and views typical of the first capital of Russia in mid-18th century.

It was a coup d'état carried out at the Imperial palace that elevated Catherine the Great to the ruler status and she was forced to stake openly her claim to the Imperial throne. Two artists were sent to Moscow with the purpose of preparing illustrations for the coronation book. The court painter Jean Louis de Vellie sketched the principal events of the coronation ceremony in September 1762 and the engraver Mikhail Makhaev filled in the architectural background in the drawings. But it was only in 1857 that the full book entitled "Drawings for the Report on the Coronation of the Empress Ekaterina Alekseevna. 1762" was finally published.

While it took about 100 years to publish the coronation book for Catherine the Great who soon lost any interest in the concept, her successors Pavel I and Aleksandr I, apparently, never envisaged producing such publications. According to the entries in the Court journals and the recollections of the contemporaries, the coronation festivities for these two Emperors were no less magnificent and well-attended events than the coronations of their predecessors. Celebrated architects and artists, for instance, Giacomo Quarenghi took part in the preparatory work. The experienced theater decorator P. Gonzago was specially invited by the Director of the Imperial Theaters Prince N.B. Yusupov who was the supervisor and the principal master of ceremonies for coronations of both Pavel I and Aleksandr I (he also oversaw the third coronation—that of Nikolai I). P. Gonzago executed many drawings of the ornaments designed for decorating the Triumphal arches and gates that were traditionally erected in the streets and thoroughfares of Moscow, especially in its central part, known as the Kitai Gorod and the Kremlin.

The tradition of publishing a coronation picture book was revived by the Emperor Nikolai I. However, the volume dedicated to the coronation of Nikolai I himself was rather modest in size and artistic value. It was published in Paris in 1828 with the subtitle "The Views of the Most Interesting Moments of the Ceremony of Coronation of Their Imperial Majesties as Painted by the Best Artists of the Nation". The volume included 14 lithographs and 7 pages of the text giving a short description of the coronation festivities. The printing quality was quite high as the lithographs were printed at the best French printing shop run by G. Engelman but the book as a whole failed to convey the magnificence and lavishness of the ceremony of the Russian Emperor's coronation.

The bulky volume commemorating the coronation of Aleksandr II was a outstanding specimen of the book art of mid-19th century. The illustrations were executed by the well-known Russian and foreign artists including the Court painter M.A. Zicci, V.F. Timm, the publisher of the journal "Russian Art Herald", the amateur painter Prince G.G. Gagarin, N.E. Sverchkov, and many other contributors.

In contrast to the coronation books published previously, in which the illustrations were separate from the text presenting the description of the coronation festivities, the book on the coronation of Aleksandr II had a different composition that was later on used for the books commemorating the coronations of Aleksandr III and Nikolai II. The book text was divided in five large chapters which presented not only a very detailed description of all events following the promulgation of the "Declaration" on April 20, 1856 stipulating the time and procedures of the coronation process. The book also described the history of the "Tsardom crowning" ritual in Russia starting with its origin traced back to the Kievan Prince Vladimir Monomakh, and gave the lists of the participants at the coronation ceremony, including the members of the Imperial Family and the envoys of foreign states. It was the first coronation book which described in detail the preparations made in Moscow for the coronation festivities. Most of the illustrations depicted Moscow views. The young Saint-Petersburg architect Ippolito Monighetti made later famous by the design of the Polytechnical Museum in Moscow, executed most of the ornaments in the book in the Russian style producing a harmoniously artistic book design. The colored illustrations in the book depicted not only the details of the coronation ceremony but practically all noteworthy events occurring in Moscow throughout the relevant period, such as celebratory dinners, receptions, military parades and displays, street pageants, and fireworks. A large illustration depicting a contemporary panoramic view of the Kremlin and Moscow was included in the book.

Aleksandr III was crowned soon after the tragic death of his father, the Emperor Aleksandr II, killed by revolutionary terrorists on March 1, 1881. The coronation book was intended to emphasize the continuity and immense authority of the Imperial power and its deep roots in the ancient history of the Russian state. To ensure the artistic excellence of the book its publisher commissioned such prominent Russian artists of the period as the Makovsky brothers—Konstantin, Vladimir, and Nikolai—Vasily Vereshchagin, Vasily Polenov, Vasily Surikov, and Ivan Kramskoy.

The artists commissioned for making drawings for the picture book on the coronation of Nikolai II were also very well-known and included Ilya Repin, Aleksandr Benois, and Valentin Serov. The two-volume book was published in 1899 under the general title "The Coronation Collection". The first volume included the contributions entitled "The Historical Review of Russian Coronations" and "The Account of the Holy Coronation of Their Imperial Majesties the Emperor Nikolai II and the Empress Aleksandra Fedorovna on May 14, 1896". The second volume contained a large number of photographs of the participants of the coronation festivities and the texts of various official documents, such as, government orders and Court guidelines, coronation declaration, decrees, and rules which were directly related to the coronation procedures.

The central decorative features of the coronation ceremonies held in the last third of the 19th century were the lighting arrangements that were extremely colorful and inventive according to the reminiscences of the spectators. Not only the Kremlin but all the main streets and thoroughfares of Moscow were flooded with brilliant lights.

In 1883—1896 the Moscow artist Vasily Rozanov executed a series of 17 unique paintings which belong now to the State History Museum in Moscow. The paintings depict views of the festively lit Moscow streets and buildings that created an especially solemn and happy atmosphere in the days when the ancient crowning rites were performed in the city. Many contemporaries would undoubtedly second the cheerful exclamation of one of the coronation ceremony spectators who wrote, "In all my life I have never experienced anything so momentous and so marvelous as that memorable day!".

186

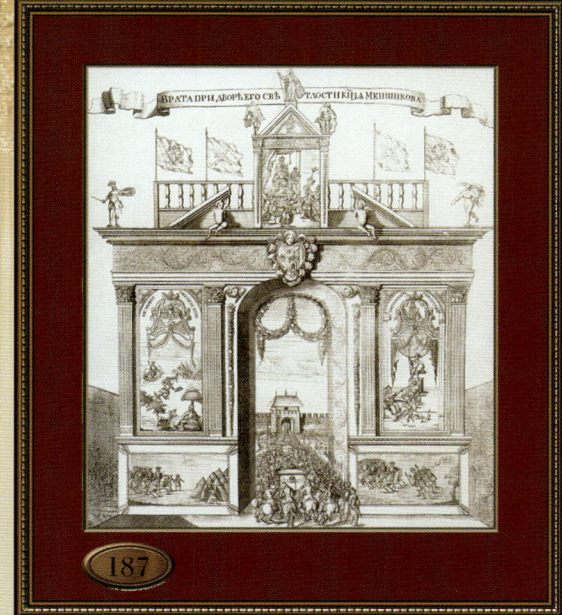

The picturesque sights of the ancient Moscow with its white-stone buildings during the coronation festivities always fascinated artists, lithographers, and engravers whose works depicted numerous Moscow scenes.

The Triumphal Arch erected by Prince Aleksandr Menshikov who was given the rank of Field-Marshal for his role during the Battle of Poltava was built near his palace in the Myasnitskaya Street near the entrance gate of the White City. The Arch was decorated with two painted panels, one showing Peter the Great with his entourage near the encampment deserted by the Swedish Army and another depicting the surrendering Swedish generals. Later the famous Red Triumphal Gate was built approximately at the same site because during the coronation festivities in the 18th century the tsar's train was passing along the Myasnitskaya Street and the Basmannaya Street on its way from the Kremlin to the Nemetskaya Sloboda and the Golovinsky Palace.

Catherine I (1684—1727) was the first Russian Empress who was crowned at the Uspensky Cathedral of the Kremlin. In November of 1723 Peter I announced his intention to crown his wife Catherine and developed a new coronation ceremony. In imitation of the ceremony of coronation for the Byzantine Emperors Peter I himself put on the Empress a diamond crown and a gold-embroidered silk ermine-fringed mantle that had been specially made for the occasion. In the period before early 18th century the Russian tsars were crowned with ceremonial shoulder robes and a crown or the "Monomakh Cap" that, according to legends, had been presented by the Byzantine Emperor Konstantin Monomakh to the Kievan Prince Vladimir. The coronation festivities were concluded with a luxurious fireworks display in the Tsarina Meadow on the bank of Moskva River opposite the Kremlin.

Peter II (1715—1730), the son of Peter's son Aleksei and Princess Charlotte Braunshweig-Wolffenbuttel, became the Emperor at the age of 12 after the death of Catherine I. On February 19, 1728, he arrived at the suburban village Vsesvyatskoe near Moscow from where he performed the ceremonial entrance to Moscow which was the first in the history of the Imperial coronations. The hunting with hounds was the main occupation of the young Emperor during his short reign. He died suddenly on February 29, 1730, on the day of his wedding to Princess Ekaterina Dolgorukova. His death resulted in discontinuation of the direct male line of the Romanov dynasty. The train of Peter II is depicted in front of the suburban estate of the Tsar Aleksei Mikhailovich which in early 18th century belonged to the Tsarina Praskovya Fedorovna, the widow of Tsar Ivan V who was a co-ruler of Russia together with Peter I. It was in the ancient wooden Izmailovo Palace that she had given birth to her younger daughter Anna who was later crowned as the Empress Anna Ioannovna of Russia.

1. ЕЯ ІМПЕРАТОРСКОЕ ВЕЛИЧЕСТВО
2. АРХІЕРЕИ НОВОГОРОЦКІИ, И ПРОЧІИ АРХІЕРЕИ
3. РЕИХСЪ КАНЦЛЕРЪ ГРАФЪ ГОЛОВКИНЪ, И ГЕНЕРАЛЪ ФЕЛДМАРШАЛЪ ДОЛГОРУКОИ
4. ГЕНЕРАЛЪ ЛУЗИНСКИИ И ГЕНЕРАЛЪ МАМОНОВЪ
5. КАВАЛЕРЫ КОТОРЫЕ НЕСЛИ РЕГАЛІИ
6. ОБЕРЪ МАРШАЛЪ И ФЕЛДМАРШАЛЪ КНЯЗЬ ГОЛИЦЫНЪ
7. ОБЕРЪ-ГОФЪ-МАРШАЛЪ ГРАФЪ ЛЕВОЛДЪ, И ГОФЪ-МАРШАЛЪ ШЕПЕЛЕВЪ
8. ОБЕРЪ ЦЕРЕМОНИ-МЕИСТЕРЪ СЪ 2 ЦЕРЕМОНИ МЕИСТЕРАМИ, И 2 ГЕРОЛДАМИ
9. МЕСТО УЧРЕЖДЕННОЕ ДЛЯ ФАМИЛИИ ЕЯ ИМПЕРАТОРСКАГО ВЕЛИЧЕСТВА
10. ИНОСТРАННЫЕ МИНИСТРЫ
11. ТРОНЪ ПОДЪ БАЛДАХИНОМЪ
12. ОБЕРЪ-ГОФЪ-МЕИСТЕРЪ И КАМЕРГЕРЫ

The interior ornamentation of the Uspensky Cathedral during the coronation of the Empress **Anna Ioannovna** (1693—1740) demonstrates the European-style opulence and the public character of the ceremony.

A special throne platform fitted with guilt guard rails and topped with a canopy was erected at the central part of the Cathedral opposite the altar. Twelve steps carpeted with the same red broadcloth with which the platform was carpeted led the Emperor's throne alongside which a table was placed for the Imperial regalia. Special galleries were erected along the cathedral walls with seats for the company observing the ceremony, that is, the members of the Imperial family, the top Russian aristocracy, the courtiers, and the foreign envoys. The assistants at the coronation ceremony shown at the side of the Empress were the Chancellor Count G. I. Golovkin and the General-Field Marshal Prince V.V. Dolgorukov. The Chief Master of Ceremonies, the well-known historian V.N. Tatishchev is shown standing at the steps.

The festivities celebrating the coronation of the Empress Anna Ioannovna were continued for seven days and accompanied with various illumination displays (the most colorful displays were held at the Nemetskaya Sloboda district), public entertainment in the streets, and fireworks. However, various entertainment events and "amusements" were carried on till the end of the year because the Empress spent the first ten months of her reign in Moscow.

The younger daughter of the great reformer of Russia Peter I, the Empress **Elizabeth** (1709—1761) took the throne on the night of November 25, 1741, as a result of a coup d'état at the court. Three months later she left the village Vsesvyatskoe on the last stage of the ceremonial entry to Moscow riding in a gilt carriage driven by eight Neapolitan horses and surrounded with an exceptionally magnificent and luxurious retinue. Four triumphal arches were erected in Moscow to greet the Empress; one of them was built at the entrance to the Golovinsky Palace, the Imperial residence at the Moscow district of Lefortovo where the Empress stayed practically all the time throughout her Moscow visit. The architect Bartolomeo Rastrelli designed two wooden palaces known as the Winter and Summer Annenhof which were built in the 1730s at the site of the former estate of Count Golovin. When preparations were made in 1742 for the coronation ceremony the two palaces were significantly enlarged by the addition of the structures called the Throne Hall, the Illumination Theater, and the Opera House and the entire ensemble was given the name of the Golovinsky Palace.

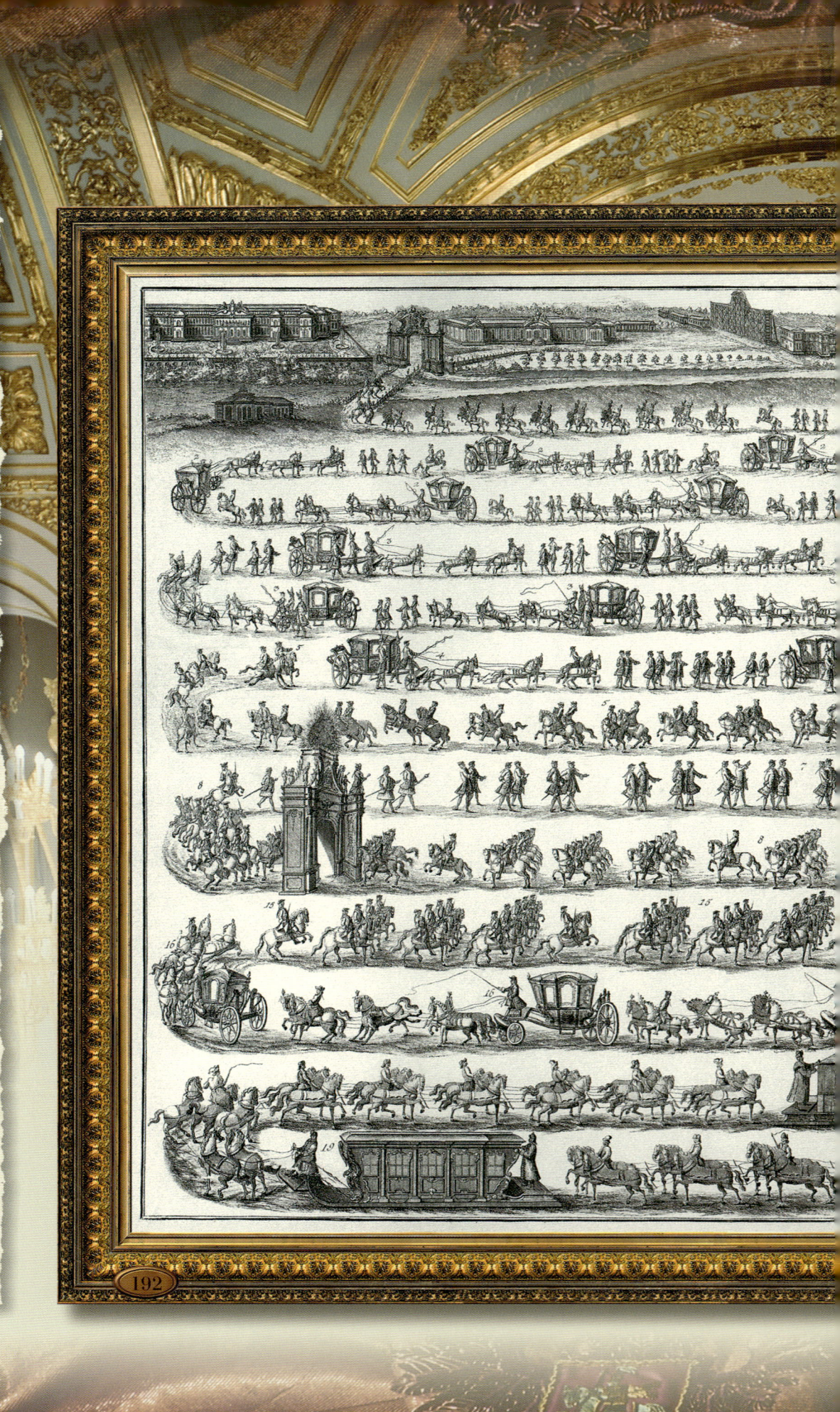

...ремонія Шествія *Ея Императорскаго Величества* въ Москву

The provision of refreshments for the populace in the streets was one of the innovations made by Peter I in the coronation procedures. Initially the refreshments were laid out at the Cathedral Square in the Kremlin. During the coronation of Pavel I there were tables laden with provisions for the populace in the Myasnitskaya Street and Lubyanskaya Square. The popular festivities in the 19th century were held at the city outskirts such as the Sokolniki park, and the Devichye and Khodynskoe fields. The holiday fare provided to people remained unchanged and consisted of whole bullocks roasted on spits and fountains squirting white and red wines.

194

An inevitable component of the coronation festivities were the worshipping trips to the most respected and prominent holy places near Moscow which were the Troitse-Sergieva Lavra monastery and the Voskresensky Monastery in the New Jerusalem religious compound which had been founded by Patriarch Nikon, the Head of the Russian Orthodox Church in 1658. The principal cathedral in the monastery was modeled on the Resurrection Church in Jerusalem. It was a very complex structure with numerous underground chapels and a magnificent stone enclosure built over the Chapel of the Holy Sepulcher. In 1723 the roof of the enclosure collapsed but it was rebuilt in 1756—1759 after the Empress Elizabeth had visited the monastery.

The Empress Elizaveta Petrovna was closely associated with Moscow. She was born at the Kolomenskoe Palace. When she was the heir to the throne she spent long periods in her country estates near Moscow at the village of Pokrovskoe and at the Aleksandrovskaya Sloboda. When she first came to Moscow in her capacity as the Empress she stayed there till the end of 1741. She took part in incessant dancing parties, fancy-dress balls, attended fireworks displays and performances by the Russian and Italian actors in the Opera House.

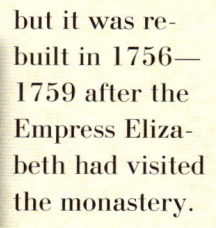

195

The Empress **Catherine II** known as the Great (1729—1796) was raised to the throne in a coup d'état on June 28, 1762, after a short reign of Peter III. Her coronation was distinguished by the especially magnificent and luxurious arrangements. A few days after the coup a Coronation Decree was promulgated and a special commission was established to prepare and run the coronation process. On September 9 the Empress arrived at the village Petrovskoe near Moscow and her ceremonial entrance into Moscow took place on September 13. The engraving depicts the reading of the Declaration of time and procedure of the coronation which was one of the central events of the coronation ceremony developed by Peter I. The Declaration was read for the first time in the Sobornaya and Ivanovskaya squares of the Kremlin and in the Red Square and then in all the principal thoroughfares of Moscow for three days.

Catherine II is depicted going down under the Imperial canopy on the Red Porch of the Faceted Chamber. Eight gentlemen-in-waiting are holding the train of her gown made of the cloth of silver. The Chancellor Count A.P. Bestuzhev-Ryumin and Count K.G. Razumovsky stand on both sides of the Empress. Special platforms carpeted with red broadcloth were installed on the Sobornaya Square leading from the Uspensky Cathedral to the Red Porch and along to the Arkhangelsky Cathedral. Horse-guardsmen were arraigned in rows along the route (the household horse-guards company was established in 1724 before the coronation of Catherine I).

In accordance with the ancient ritual of "Tsar crowning" established by the Russian Orthodox Church the Empress was anointed with myrrh and presented with the regalia of monarchy; after that the Arch-Bishop of Novgorod Dmitry brought her into the altar of the Uspensky Cathedral where he performed the Holy Communion priesthood rites. Catherine II placed the crown on her head and the Imperial mantle on her shoulders with her own hands as the Empress Elizabeth had done during her coronation.

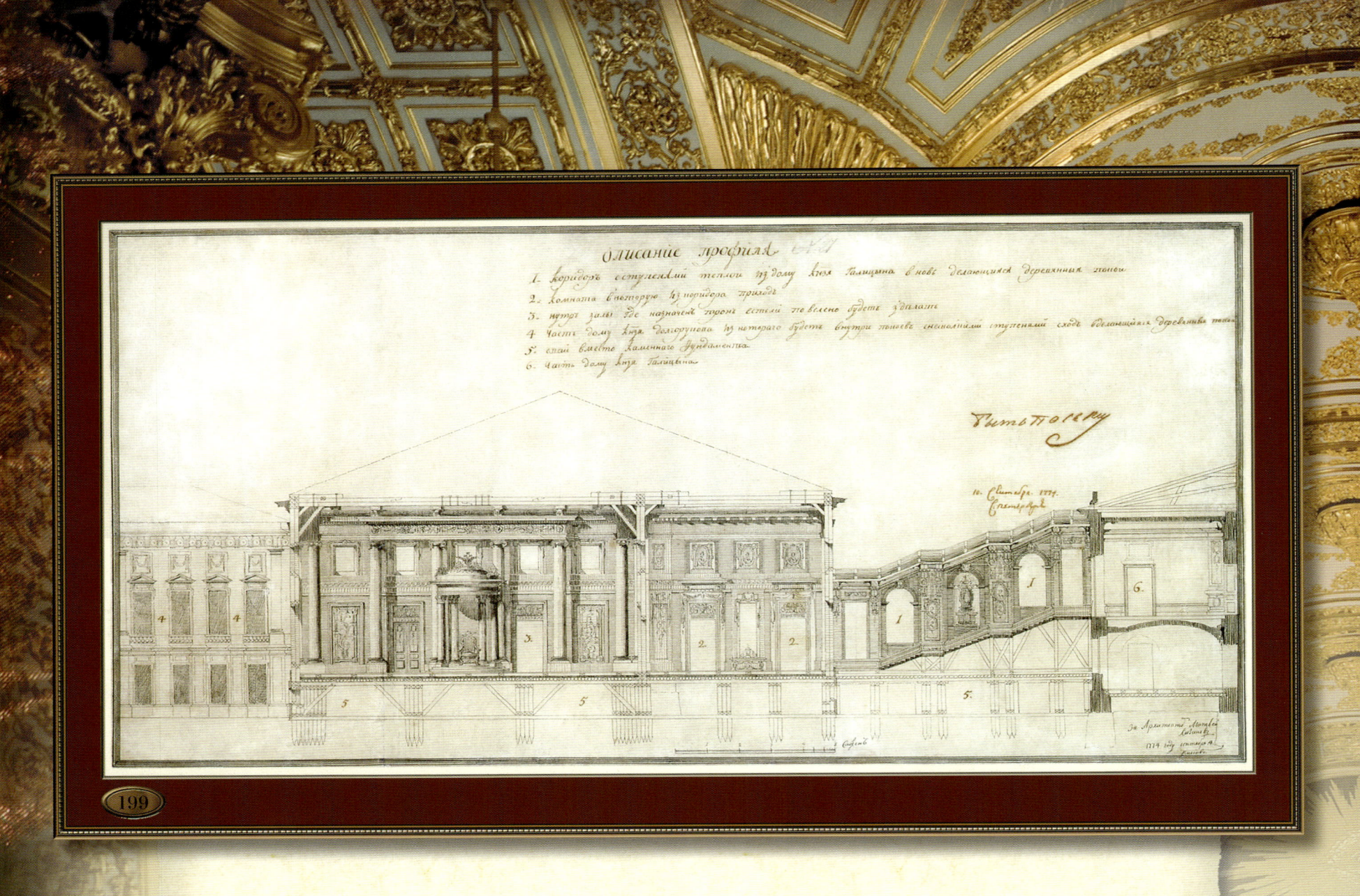

In 1775 Moscow celebrated the signing of the Kyuchuk-Kainardzhi peace treaty that marked the victory of Russia in the first war between Russia and Turkey. Since all the Imperial palaces were in the state of disrepair Catherine II gave the order to build a temporary palace for herself in the Volkhonka Street. Architect Kazakov had little time to act on the royal order and joined together two existing buildings with a wooden structure accommodating the Throne room and other ceremonial chambers. The resulting edifice was called the Prechistensky Palace and the Empress spent practically the entire year in it with the exception of the summer months. The drawing bears the longhand inscription made by Catherine II "Get it done".

The Petrovsky Travel Palace was build by architect Kazakov in 1775—1782 by an order of Catherine II. The palace was located at the distance of three versts along the Saint-Petersburg highway from the Moscow gate. The Empress visited her new suburban residence for the first time in 1785. In future all the Russian Emperors starting with Pavel I stayed at the Petrovsky Palace before making a ceremonial entrance into Moscow.

The Emperor **Pavel I** (1754—1801) made a ceremonial entrance to Moscow before his coronation on the Palm Sunday that was March 27, 1797. After visiting the Kremlin and making the traditional round of the Kremlin cathedrals the Emperor's family went to the so-called Slobodskoy Palace in the Nemetskaya Sloboda where they spent some time before moving over to the Kremlin. This palace was built in mid-18th century by Count A.P. Bestuzhev-Ryumin. In 1787 Catherine gave it away as a gift to the Chancellor A.A. Bezborodko. In the late 1796—early 1797 the palace was refurbished by Kazakov in order to adapt it for accommodating the large Emperor's family. During the coronation festival the palace was occupied by the court of the heir to the throne, the Grand Duke Aleksandr Pavlovich. When Aleksandr I came to Moscow for his coronation in 1801 he also stayed at the Slobodskoy Palace. A part of the Emperor's family stayed at the Lefortovo Palace while the Grand Duke Konstantin Pavlovich took the Old Senate building opposite the Slobodskoy Palace. Later Prince Bezborodko sold the palace to the government; in the great Moscow fire of 1812 the palace burned down and in 1827—1830 it was restored and used as the State Orphanage.

The ensemble of the Spaso-Vifansky Monastery was created in 1783—1787 and "designed and paid for" by the famous Moscow Metropolitan Platon. The monastery buildings included the Cathedral of Transfiguration of Our Lord with the Church of Resurrection of Lazarus, the residence of the Metropolitan and the monk cells. Emperor Pavel I visited Metropolitan Platon at the monastery in 1797. Emperor Aleksandr I also visited the monastery in September of 1801. Metropolitan Platon performed the religious rites for the coronations of both Pavel I and his son Aleksandr I.

Aleksandr I (1777—1825) was proclaimed Emperor on March 12, 1801 after a rumored assassination of his father. His ceremonial entry to Moscow for the coronation took place on September 1801. Troops of the horseguards regiments were positioned along the route of the tsar's convoy from the Petrovsky Palace to the Slobodskoy Palace. Special stands for the spectators and the Triumphal Arches were erected in the Tverskaya Street leading to the Kremlin. One of the arches was built at the Strastnaya Square at the site of the gate in the city wall that had been demolished in the 1770s.

The Troitse-Sergieva Lavra monastery established by Saint Sergii of Radonezh in mid-14th century is the most respected sacred site of the Russian Orthodox Church near Moscow. All Russian emperors without any exception visited it. In late 17th century tsar's residence was built in the monastery compound specially for accommodating royal visitors; the palace is depicted in the background of the water color. A decorated column commemorating the visit of Catherine the Great to the monastery is to the left of the bell tower.

In October 1817 a foundation stone was laid on the Vorobievy Hills for the temple to be built to a design by Aleksandr Vitberg in commemoration of the victory of Russia in the Patriotic War of 1812. The foundation ceremony was attended by the Emperor Aleksandr I, the Empresses Elizaveta and Maria, the Grand Dukes Mikhail and Nikolai (the latter was accompanied by his wife, the Grand Duchess Aleksandra), and the Crown Prince Wilhelm of Prussia.

After the liturgy service held at the Our Lady of Tikhvin church near the Novodevichy Convent had been completed the sacred procession went across the Moskva River over a temporary bridge to the foundation site. The streets Mokhovaya and Prechistenka leading from the Kremlin to the Devichy Field and then to the Vorobievy Hills were lined with the troops of the Imperial guards regiments.

In August 1816 the Emperor Aleksandr I came for the first time since the Patriotic War of 1812 to Moscow where the restoration work was still continued after the devastation of the great fires caused by the French occupation in 1812. On August 15 he was accompanied by his brother Grand Duke Nikolai at a service in the Uspensky Cathedral. On the next day Aleksandr I addressed an assembly of the Moscow gentry saying, "I am happy, gentlemen, we have met again in Moscow after the hard times and our heavy labors. … we have earned glory from all the nations. We have saved Russia and at the same time we have saved Europe, too."

The Emperor **Nikolai I** (1796—1855) made the ceremonial entrance into Moscow on July 25, 1826, soon after the he had approved the harsh court sentences to the participants of the December 1825 rebellion against the Russian monarchy. Three days before the coronation public readings of the Declaration on the coronation time and procedures were made in the streets and public places of Moscow. Traditionally, the Declaration was read out by the Senate secretaries accompanied by the heralds, trumpeters, and kettle-drummers, supervised by senor courtiers— Chief Masters of ceremonies Prince Gagarin and Count Vorontsov-Dashkov, and guarded by two squads of the Court horse-guardsmen.

The coronation of Nikolai I and the Empress Aleksandra Fedorovna was performed on August 22. The crowning ritual was performed by the senior Holy Synod member Serafim, the Metropolitan of Novgorod, whose assistants in the ceremony were Evgeny, the Metropolitan of Kiev, and Filaret, the Metropolitan of Moscow.
The Emperor Nikolai I is depicted wearing the mantle and crown at the Northern gate of the Uspensky Cathedral, next to him are his brothers, the Grand Dukes Konstantin and Mikhail, and then the Empress Aleksandra Fedorovna and the dowager Empress Maria Fedorovna. In accordance with the ancient tradition, after the coronation the Emperor went to visit the Arkhangelsky and Blagoveshchensky Cathedrals before returning to the Kremlin Palace.

The Emperor Nikolai I visited the Neskuchny estate of the Countess A.A Orlova. in a Moscow suburb for the first time in 1826 when he came to Moscow for his coronation. In 1832 the estate was purchased for the Empress Aleksandra and was named the Aleksandrinsky Summer Palace or Aleksandriya. When the Emperors Aleksandr III and Nikolai II arrived to Moscow for their coronations they stayed in this palace. In mid-18th century the estate was the property of the immensely rich industrialist P.A. Demidov and the splendid botanical garden cultivated in it was famous throughout Russia. The Moscow architect E.D. Tyurin redecorated the estate in the 1830s after it had been designated as a Court country palace.

Nikolai I was often making prolonged inspection tours over all Russia. In 1837 his carriage broke down and collapsed in a road near the town of Chembary. The Emperor suffered a broken collar bone in the accident. Count A. Benkendorf, the head of the Russian secret service and his close aide accompanying him in the trip, noted, "After coming to Moscow the Emperor sat in the carriage alone to give more room to his damaged arm, when traveling throughout the entire Moscow from the Kolomensky Palace to the Aleksandrinsky Palace."

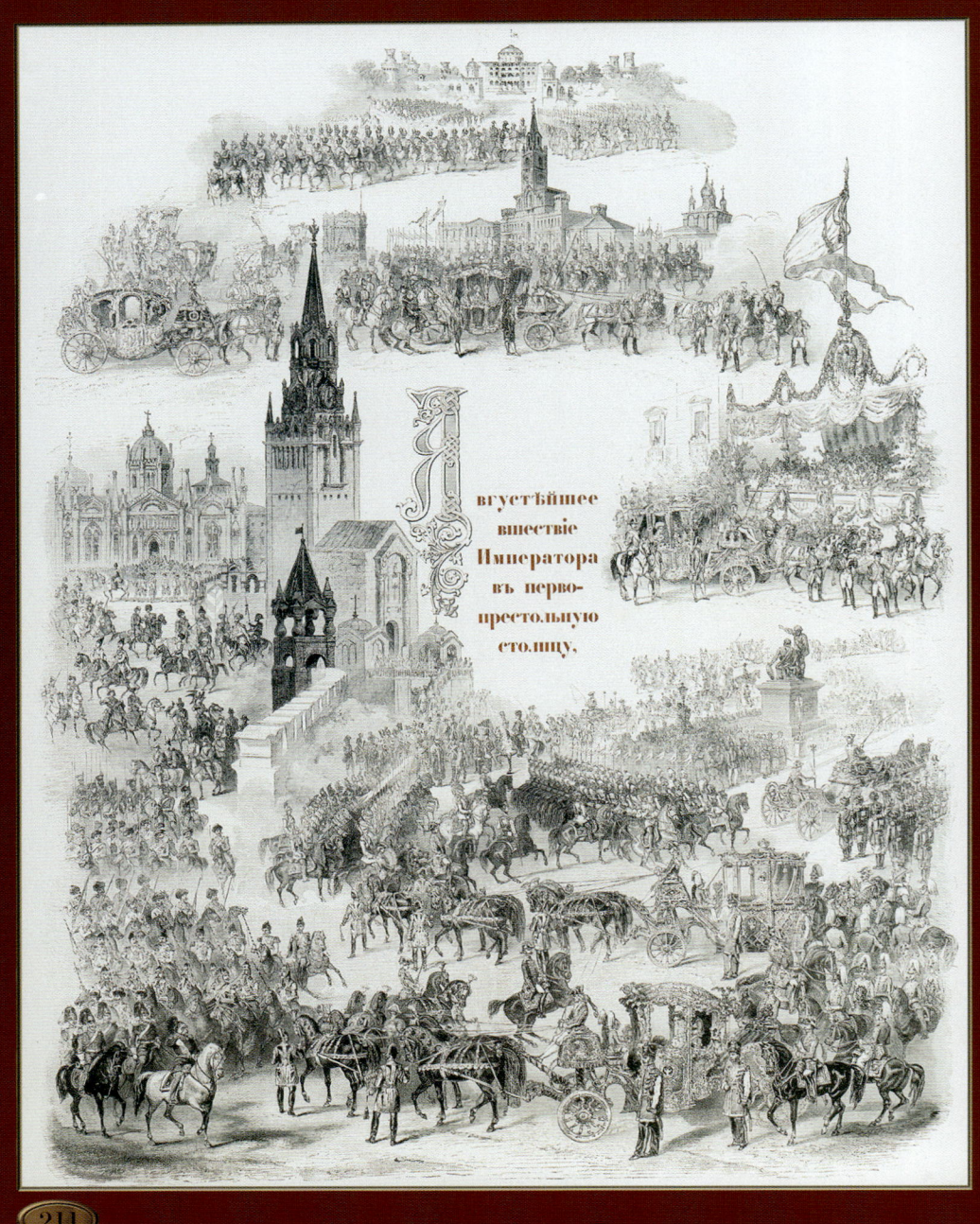

The coronation of the Emperor **Aleksandr II** (1818—1881) and the Empress Maria Aleksandrovna was performed on August 26, 1856. The coronation procession started at the Petrovsky Palace at 3 p.m. accompanied with the ringing of church bell and a gun salute of 71 salvos. The procession included the members of the royal family, the senior courtiers, and the household companies of the horse-guards regiments. The Emperor was riding a grey mount and was accompanied with his sons—the heir to the throne Grand Duke Nikolai and the Grand Duke Aleksandr, the brothers of the Emperor Nikolai I the Grand Dukes Konstantin, Nikolai and Mikhail, Prince P.G. Oldenburg, and the Aide-de-Camp Generals of the Imperial Court. The gilded 18th-century carriages carried the dowager Empress Aleksandra Fedorovna, the Empress Maria with her son Vladimir, and the Grand Duchesses Maria Pavlovna, Aleksandra Iosifovna, Elena Pavlovna, and Maria Nikolaevna.

Pavel I was the first Russian Emperor who had the coronation of himself and his wife performed in the same event. After Pavel I had crowned himself he placed the smaller Imperial crown, the Imperial mantle, and the diamond-studded chain of the Order of Saint Andrew on the Empress with his own hands. The Empress Maria Aleksandrovna is depicted kneeling before the Emperor. Standing next to her are her assistants, her brother Prince Aleksandr of Hessen, and Duke Georg Mecklenburgh. The ladies in ethnic Russian costumes and folk head-dresses accommodated in the galleries in the Uspensky Cathedral shown in the picture are ladies-in-waiting at the Imperial Court.

A ceremonial dinner was traditionally held at the ancient Faceted Chamber of the Kremlin after the completion of the coronation ritual. Present at the dinner were the members of the State Council, senior priests of the Russian Orthodox Church, members of the higher aristocracy, senior functionaries of the Imperial Court and the ladies-in-waiting. A separate table under a canopy was set for the family of Aleksandr II; the Empress Maria Aleksandrovna was seated to the left of the Emperor, and the dowager Empress Aleksandra Fedorovna to the right of him. The chairs used at the coronation ceremony were brought over from the Uspensky Cathedral; Aleksandr II had the ivory throne manufactured for Tsar Ivan III and the two Empresses were seated at the thrones that had been made for the tsars Mikhail and Aleksei Romanov. The ancient plates, utensils, and silverware stored at the Armory Chamber of the Kremlin were used throughout the dinner.

In the first three days after the coronation the Emperor was holding court in the Andreevsky Hall in the Kremlin receiving congratulations from the members of the State Council, the Holy Synod, the Senate, diplomats, and elected representatives of all the estates of the Russian nation. The delegates of the Cossack forces were introduced by the heir to the throne Nikolai Aleksandrovich (1843—1865) who held the title of the Sovereign Chieftain of all the Cossack forces. The younger sons of Aleksandr II including the future Emperor Aleksandr III were also present at the ceremonies.

The program of the coronation festivities included attendance at a ceremonial performance at the Bolshoi Theater in addition to a variety of balls, receptions and official dinners. The painting shows the ceremonial train of Aleksandr II and the Empress Maria for the Bolshoi Theater passing through the Voskresensky Gate of the Kitai-Gorod on August 30. The entire city was illuminated with colored lights on that night as it was on the coronation day.

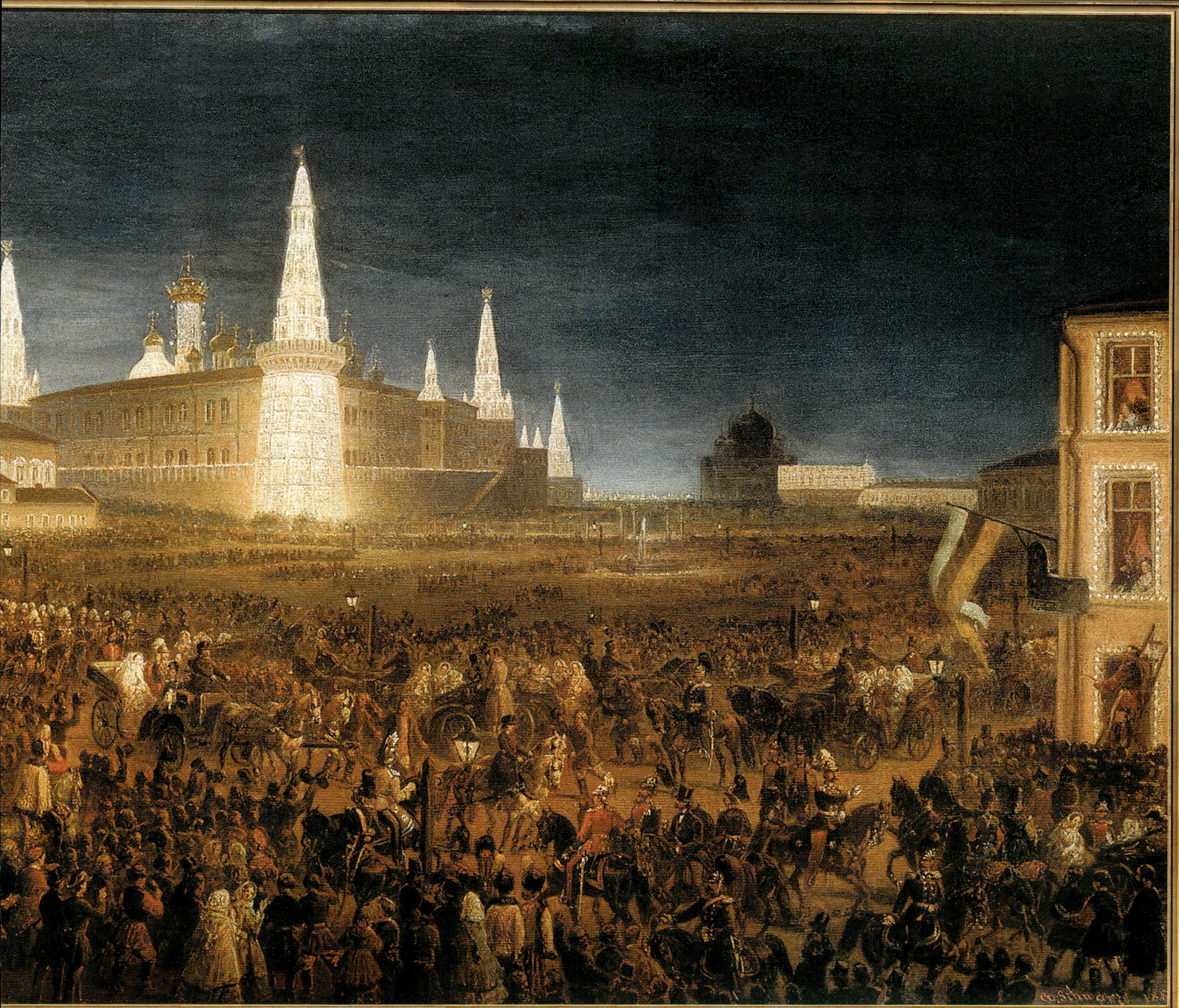

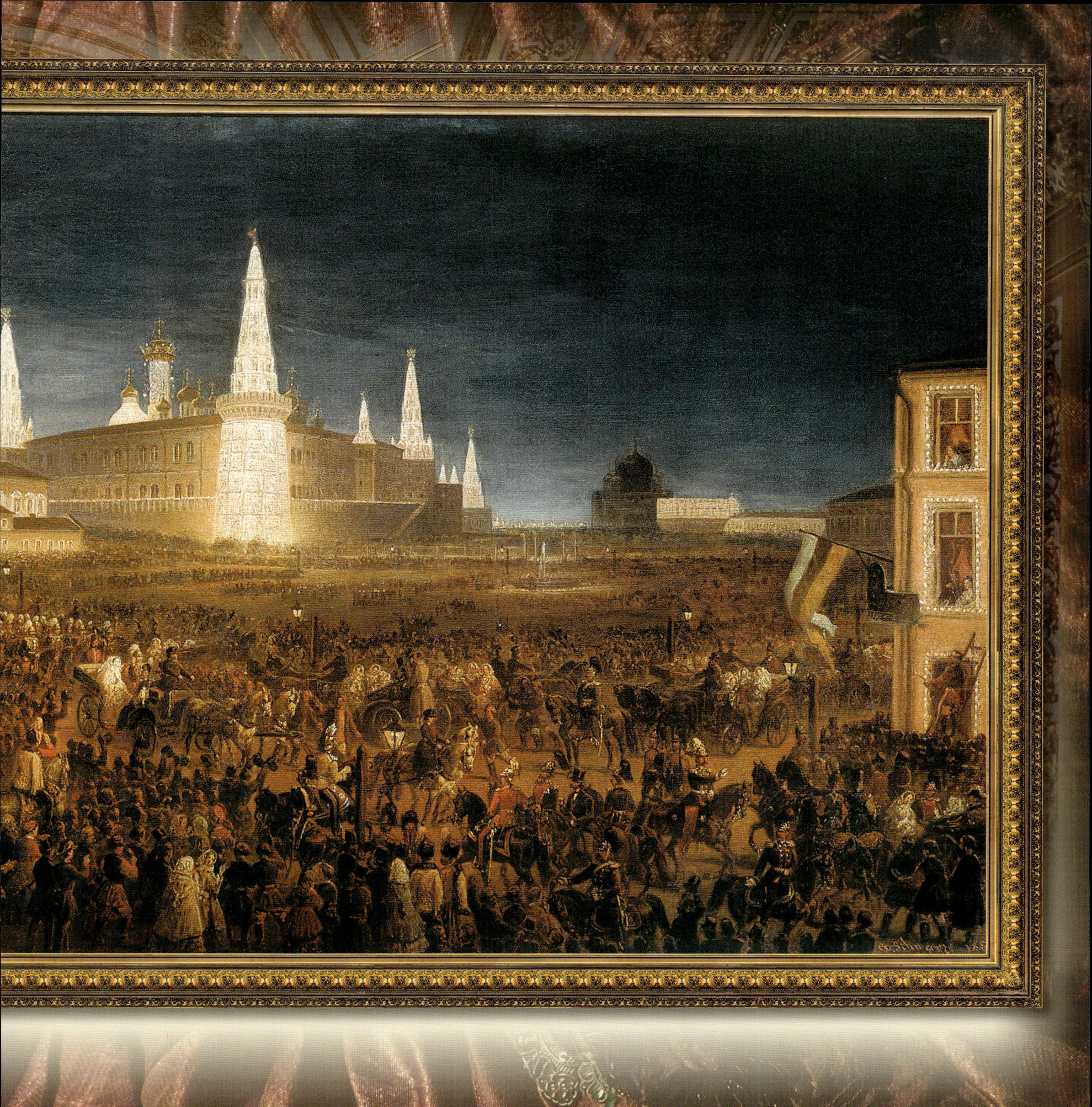

The coronation procession of Aleksandr II between the Uspensky Cathedral and the Arkhangelsky Cathedral was greeted with 101 salvos of the canons placed in a row at the top of the Kremlin Hill. To the right of the Ivan the Great bell tower one can see the buildings of the Chudov monastery (founded in the 14th century) and the smaller Nikolaevsky Palace in which the Emperor was born in April 1818. The temporary wooden pavilions built for the spectators in the square were designed in the Russian decorative style. Special illumination structures were installed on the Ivan the Great bell tower. Scenes of the Aleksandr II coronation ceremony were depicted in a number of paintings executed by the German painter Gustav Schwarz.

Before the coronation day the Emperor and his family traditionally spent some time in a hideaway outside the Kremlin. In 1856 Aleksandr II found refuge in Ostankino, the famous suburban estate of the Count Sheremetev. The Emperor spent about a week in the estate and only the members of his immediate family were allowed to visit him there. Emperor's retinue were accommodated in 12 country cottages near the estate. In 1797 Count N.P. Sheremetev gave a reception for Emperor Pavel I in the Ostankino Palace (built in 1792—1798) during the coronation festivities.

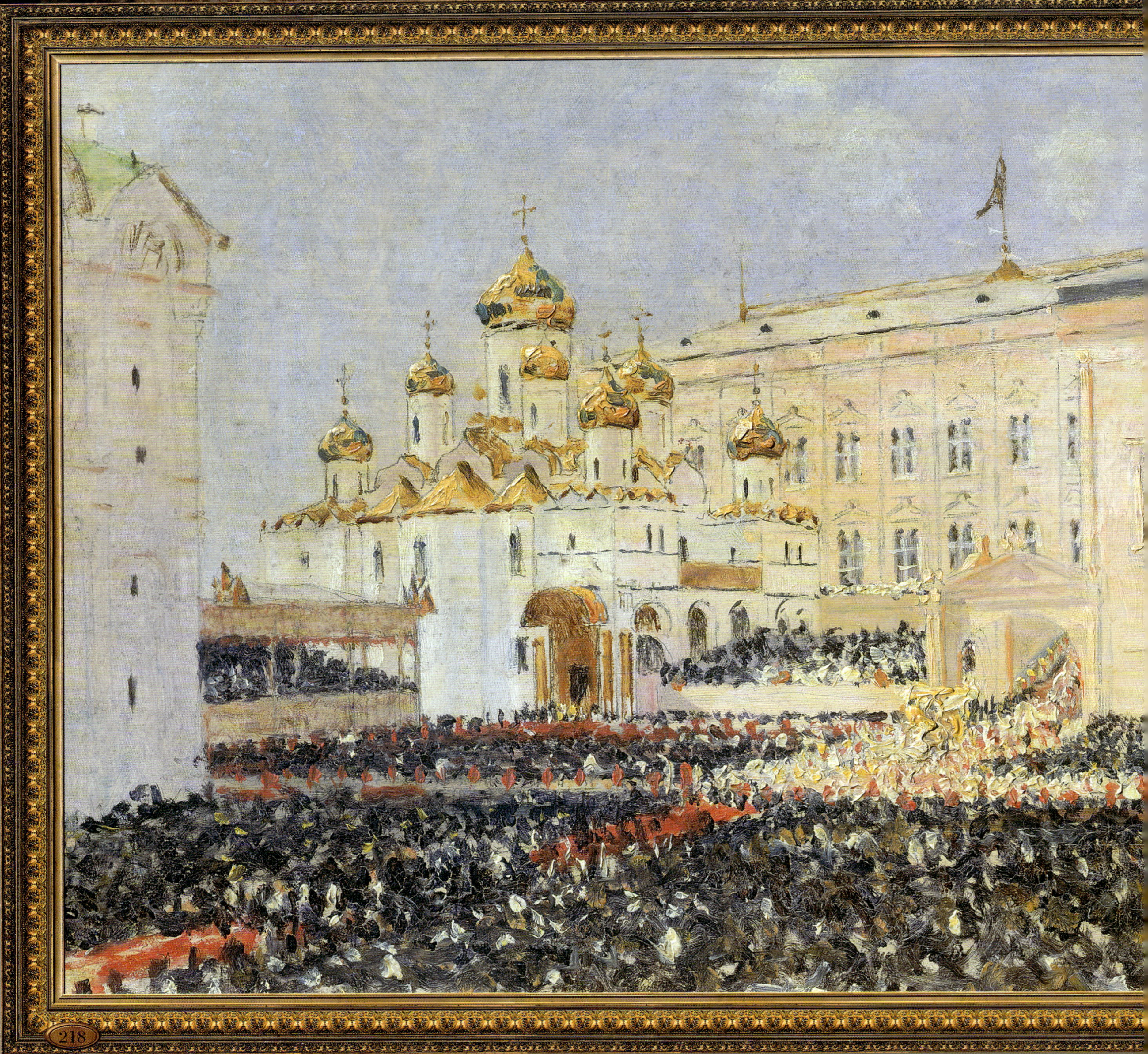

218

The coronation of the Emperor **Aleksandr III** (1845—1894) was performed on May 15, 1883 almost two years after the terrorist assassination of Aleksandr II. The new Emperor attached a special importance to the coronation event which he believed to be a factor of an extreme political significance. The coronation ceremony was attended by the representatives of the Russian cities and towns, local communities, and various public organizations and government agencies.

As stipulated by the coronation procedure, the principal Imperial regalia, that is, the mantle, the diamond-studded star and chain of the Order of Saint Andrew, the major and minor Imperial crowns, the scepter, the orb, and the sword of state, were ceremoniously transferred from the Kremlin Palace to the Uspensky Cathedral (before the Emperor emerged into the Sobornaya square). The Imperial ensign and the coat of arms are over the thrones of the Emperor and Empress.

The most important moment of the Aleksandr III coronation ceremony was when the highest-ranking member of the Holy Synod performed the crowning ritual. The Metropolitan of Novgorod Isidor offers the major Imperial crown on a cushion to the Emperor who stands before the throne wearing a mantle with the diamond-studded star of the Order of Saint Andrew. Standing on the left behind the throne is the commanding officer of the Horse Guards holding a naked broadsword.

220

Christ the Savior Cathedral designed by Konstantin Ton was built near the Kremlin in commemoration of the victory of Russia in the Patriotic War of 1812. On May 26, 1883, during the coronation festivities the Cathedral was consecrated in the presence of Aleksandr III.

The coronation illumination displays were first lit in the evening of May 15, 1883. The displays were designed by Fabritsius, a lieutenant-colonel of the Engineering Corps and the artist P.S. Boitsov and the circuits were installed under the command of N.I. Radivanovsky, a captain of the Technical Galvanic Department of the Engineering Corps. M.F. Shishkin, the supervisor of artificial illumination of the Imperial Theaters, participated in the preparatory activities for designing the illumination displays. The illumination of the Kremlin was particularly impressive. The walls and towers were lit up with garlands of thousands of special lights and the Ivan the Great bell tower was decorated with a crown of the multi-colored sparkler fireworks. Rotating electric spotlights were mounted on the spires of the Kremlin towers.

Aleksandr III went to a performance at the Bolshoi Theater on May 18, 1883. The performance included the first part and the finale of M.I. Glinka's opera "Life for the Tsar", and a new Petipa's ballet "Day and Night". The retinue of Aleksandr III and Empress Maria was comprised of the members of the Imperial family including Emperor's sons, the Grand Dukes Sergei, Vladimir, and Aleksei (the latter two are standing to the right of the Emperor), the Grand Dukes Konstantin Nikolaevich (he is sitting in the first row on the right wearing admiral's uniform) and Mikhail Nikolaevich wearing field-marshal's uniform; the Grand Duchesses Olga Fedorovna, Aleksandra Iosifovna, and Maria Pavlovna; the Greek Queen Olga Konstantinovna (she is sitting to the left of the Empress), the Duchess of Edinburgh, and Maria Aleksandrovna, the younger sister of the Emperor. To the right of the Empress is her brother Valdemar, the heir to the throne of Danmark.

The festivities commemorating the coronation of **Nikolai II** (1868—1918) were the last in the history of the Russian Empire, they were fairly short in duration and lasted from May 9 to 26, 1896. Nikolai II accompanied by his wife Aleksandra Fedorovna and numerous courtiers and aides embarked on the traditional walk to the Uspensky Cathedral where the coronation ceremony was to be held. After the coronation the procession headed by the Emperor went to the Arkhangelsky Cathedral to pay homage to the graves of the ancestors and then to the Blagoveshchensky Cathedral from where the Emperor went up to the Red Porch and greeted the crowds collected in the Kremlin squares.

The water color depicts the ceremonial procession of the Emperor Nikolai II and the Empress Aleksandra from the Kremlin Palace to the Uspensky Cathedral during a visit of the tsar's family to Moscow in early 1900s.

225

226

The Emperor Nikolai II wearing the uniform of the Preobrazhensky Guards Regiment and the mantle is shown at the most meaningful instant of the coronation ceremony. He is accepting the crown presented to him by Pallady, the Metropolitan of Saint-Petersburg. The Grand Dukes, Vladimir and Mikhail (the younger brother of the Emperor) are standing to the right of Nikolai II. The Empress is wearing a silver brocade gown and the ribbon of the Order of Saint Catherine. Next to her are the Grand Dukes Sergei and Pavel. The dowager Empress Maria Fedorovna is at the left of the throne enclosure. Standing on the stair steps are the senior government officials and the commanding officer of the Household Horsemen Guards Regiment with a naked broadsword and his helmet in his hands.

A large number of pavilions for the spectators were erected along the Tverskaya Street and at other public sites along the route of the ceremonial Emperor's procession. In the evenings the pavilions were gaudily illuminated with multitudes of colored electric light bulbs.

227

The Kremlin was flooded with lights of the illumination displays during the coronation festivities of 1896. Up to 200 000 electric lamps of the blue, green, white, and golden-yellow colors were installed on the Kremlin walls and towers and the Ivan the Great bell tower. Searchlights were installed on the Kremlin tower tops. Thousands of people enjoying the illumination displays thronged the streets of Moscow and the Kremlin where the view was especially spectacular.

On May 18 Nikolai II and Empress Aleksandra visited the popular festival site at the Khodynskoe Field and then went to the Petrovsky Palace where they received representatives of the "millions living in the countryside", that is, the landed gentry, the rural local administrators, and the Cossack chieftains. The elected leader of the gentry of the Moscow Province Prince Trubetskoy delivered a speech of greetings. Then the Emperor entertained the rural administrators at a special celebratory dinner.

226

On May 22, 1896 Nikolai II accompanied by Empress Aleksandra, Dowager Empress Maria, and other family members paid a visit to the Troitse-Sergieva Lavra monastery. After the special church service conducted at the Troitsky Cathedral the Emperor went to the Gefsimansky Skit, the monastic retreat of Filaret, the famous Moscow Metropolitan.

List of illustrations

1. Monument of Peter the Great at the Senatskaya Square. Unknown artist. 1820s. Lithograph, colored print. SPM

2. The grand staircase in the Winter Palace. F. Kellerhoven from the original painting by V.S. Sadovnikov. 1858. Chromolithograph. SPM

3. Martial parade at the Winter Palace. V.S. Sadovnikov. 1840s. Water colors on paper

4. The Winter Palace. F. Perrot. After 1850. Colored lithograph. SPM

5. Larger church in the Winter Palace F. Kellerhoven from the original painting by V.S. Sadovnikov. 1858. Chromolithograph. SPM

6. Georgievsky throne stateroom in the Winter Palace. J.-R. Lemercier from the original painting by V.S. Sadovnikov. 1858. Chromolithograph. SPM

7. Field-Marshals' Stateroom in the Winter Palace. J.-R. Lemercier from the original painting by V.S. Sadovnikov. 1858. Chromolithograph. SPM

8. The portrait gallery of war heroes in the Winter Palace. J.-R. Lemercier from the original painting by V.S. Sadovnikov. 1858. Chromolithograph. SPM

9. View of the archway at the General Staff building. P.A. Aleksandrov. 1825. Colored lithograph. SPM

10. View through the archway in the General Staff building. L.-J. Arnout. 1840s. Lithograph, colored print. SPM

11. The Dvortsovaya Embankment. View from Neva. K.P. Beggrow. 1837. Lithograph, water colors. SPM

12. View of the Tavrichesky Palace from the Neva River. Unknown artist. 1825. Lithograph. SPM

13. Panorama of Neva with a view of the Admiralty. Copy of engraving by E.G. Vinogradov from the original drawing by M.I. Makhaev. 1753. Engraving, water colors. SPM

14. View of Neva at the Mining Institute. I.W. Barth. 1810s. Water colors, gouache on paper. SPM

15. View of the Dvortsovaya Embankment from the Petropavlovskaya Fortress. B. Paterssen. 1806. Engraving, water colors. SPM

16. View of the Marble Palace and the Summer Garden from the Petropavlovskaya Fortress. B. Paterssen. 1806. Engraving, water colors. SPM

17. View of the Marble Palace from the Petropavlovskaya Fortress. K.G. Hammer from the original by Rittner. 1808. Engraving, water colors. SPM

18. View of the Admiralty and the St. Isaac's Cathedral. P.A. Aleksandrov. 1825. Colored lithograph. SPM

19. Stock Exchange designed by Quarenghi. J.-B. de la Traverse. 1787. Paper, gouache, water colors. SPM

20. View of the Saint-Petersburg Stock Exchange and its environs. I.A. Ivanov from his own original drawing. 1814. Engraving, water colors. SPM

21. Saint-Petersburg Stock Exchange. From the original drawing by B. Paterssen. 1807. Engraving, water colors. SPM

22. Trooping the colors at the horse-guards Manege in Saint-Petersburg. Unknown artist. 1820s. Water colors, ceruse on paper. SPM

23. View of the Mars Field and the Summer Garden. Unknown artist. 1810s. Aquatint etching. SPM

24. View of the Petropavlovskaya Fortress. M.F. Damam-Demartret. 1800. Water colors, gouache, Indian ink on paper. SPM

25. View of Neva from the Petropavlovskaya Fortress. S.F. Galaktionov. 1821. Colored lithograph. SPM

26. Boating for entertainment. J.A. Atkinson. 1804. Varnish, aquatint, water colors. SPM

27. Mikhailovsky Palace. Dvortsovaya Embankment. L.J. Jacottet and Ch. Bachelier from the original by I.J. Charlemagne. 1850s. Colored lithograph. SPM

28. View of the Hermitage Theater from the Vasilievsky Island. Unknown artist. 1824—1827. Lithograph. SPM

29. View of the Hermitage Bridge. Unknown artist. 1820s. Colored lithograph. SPM

30. View of the Angliiskaya Embankment. L.J. Jacottet from the original by I.J. Charlemagne. 1850s. Colored lithograph. SPM

31. View of the Angliiskaya Embankment. F. Martens. Early 19th century. Aquatint etching. SPM

32. View of the Neva Embankment at the Summer Garden. Unknown artist. 1822. Colored lithograph. SPM

33. Sledge sliding from ice hills on Neva in the Lent festival. M.F. Damam-Demartret. Early 19th century. Water colors, Indian ink on paper. SPM

34. Skating on Neva. E.M. Korneev. 1820s. Etching, aquatint, colored print. SPM

35. Ice mountains on the Tsaritsinsky Meadow. Unknown artist. 1850s. Chromolithograph. SPM

36. View of the old Anichkov Bridge and Naryshkin's townhouse on the Fontanka River. P.A. Aleksandrov. 1825. Colored lithograph. SPM

37. View of the Nikolo-Bogoyavlensky Marine Cathedral from Yekaterininsky canal. From the original by F. Perrot. 1839—1840. Lithograph, colored print. SPM

38. Fontanka. View downstream from the garden of the Yusupov Palace. From the original by F. Perrot. 1839—1840. Lithograph, colored print. SPM

39. View to the Academy of Arts. From the original by F. Perrot. 1839—1840. Lithograph, colored print. SPM

40. View to the Mikhailovsky Palace from the garden on the square. H. Chevalier and Smidt from the original by I.J. Charlemagne. 1850s. Lithograph. SPM

41. Panorama of the Nevsky Prospekt from the Police Bridge. K.P. Beggrow. 1837. Engraving, water colors. SPM

42. Admiralty. K.P. Beggrow. 1837. Colored lithograph. SPM

43. View to the Catholic church (Saint Catherine's Catholic Church) and the Mikhailovskaya Street. L.J. Jacottet and G.L. Regamey from the original by I.J. Charlemagne. 1850s. Lithograph, colored print. SPM

44. Sennaya Square. L-.J. Arnout. After 1850. Lithograph, colored print. SPM

45. The Nevsky Prospect. K.P. Beggrow. 1837. Colored lithograph. SPM

46. The Kazansky Cathedral. K.P. Beggrow. 1837. Engraving, water colors. SPM

47. The Kazansky Cathedral. L.-J. Arnout. After 1850. Lithograph, colored print. SPM.

48. View to Neva and the Pontoon Bridge. Unknown painter. 1820s. Lithograph. SPM

49. The Saint Isaacs Pontoon Bridge. L.P.A. Bichebois. After 1850. Lithograph, colored print. SPM

50. The Saint Isaacs Cathedral. Ph. Benois. After 1855. Colored lithograph. SPM

51. The Bolshoy Kamenny Theatre. Nuri from the original drawing by F. Dietz. 1840s. Lithograph. SPM

52. Sledge sliding. J.A. Atkinson. 1803. Aquatint, water colors. SPM

53. Emperor Nikolai I. From the original by Schmidt. 1830s. Lithograph. SLM

54. The Public Library. Panorama of the Nevsky Prospect. I.A.Ivanov from the original drawing of V.S. Sadovnikov. 1830s. Colored lithograph. SPM

55. The Aleksandrinsky Theatre. K.P. Beggrow. 1837. Colored lithograph. SPM

56. The Bolshoy Kamenny Theater. B. Paterssen. 1806. Engraving, water colors. SPM

57. The Paris fashions. The fashion picture from the magazine "Common Talk". 1831

58. The Smolny monastery. E. Gostein. 1840s. Colored lithograph. SPM

59. The Aleksandro-Nevskaya Lavra monastery. Unknown painter. 1820s. Colored lithograph. SPM

60. View to Naryshkin's summer house on Aptekarsky Island. P.A. Aleksandrov. 1824. Colored lithograph. SPM

61. Stagecoach station. The coach shed. L. Premazzi. 1848. Gouache, water colors, Indian ink on paper. SHM

62. Stagecoach station. Platform. L. Premazzi. 1848. Gouache, water colors, Indian ink on paper. SHM

63. Stagecoach station. View of the waiting-room. L. Premazzi. 1848. Gouache, water colors, Indian ink on paper. SHM

64. Opening of the Saint-Petersburg-Pavlovsk railroad. K.P. Beggrow. 1837. Colored lithograph. SPM

65. Tsarskoe Selo Railroad in Saint-Petersburg. Unknown artist. Mid-19th century. Pencil on paper. SLM

66. Saint-Petersburg railroad. September 12, 1852. Cheap popular print. SHM

67. Gallery of Saint-Petersburg passenger station. A. Petzold. 1851. Water colors on paper. RSL

68. Saint-Petersburg passenger railroad station. A. Petzold. 1851. Water colors on paper. RSL

69. Courtyard of the Saint-Petersburg passenger railroad station; view from the Saint-Petersburg Gate. A. Petzold. 1851. Water colors on paper. RSL

70. View of the Ekateringof bridge over the river Ekateringofka. 1824. Lithograph. SPM

71. Railroad station and the French restaurant in the Ekateringof park. Unknown artist. 1824. Colored lithograph. SPM

72. New bridge to the Peter I palace in the Ekateringof park. Unknown artist. 1824. Colored lithograph. SPM

73. Café in the Ekateringof park. Unknown artist. 1824. Colored lithograph. SPM

74. Russian cab. B.-E. Swebach. 1830s. Colored lithograph. SPM

75. Cottage in Aleksandria. K.P. Beggrow. 1837. Engraving, water colors. SPM

76. Monplaisir in the Petergof. K.P. Beggrow. 1837. Engraving, water colors. SPM

77. View of the Pavlovsk palace. A.E. Martynov. 1820s. Lithograph. SPM

78. One day in Pavlovsk. Temple of the Friendship. From the original by Aubrun. 1823. Lithograph. SPM

79. Pavlovsk railroad station. Unknown artist. 1830s. Engraving, water colors. SPM

80. Tsarskoe Selo. A.E. Martynov.1821. Colored lithograph. SPM

81. View of the Tsarskoe Selo park. A.E. Martynov. 1821. Colored lithograph. SPM

82. View of the Tsarskoe Selo palace. A.E. Martynov. 1821. Colored lithograph. SPM

83. View of the Lyceum, Ekaterininsky Palace church and a part of the greenhouse. K.K. Schulz from the original by J.G. Meyr. 1844. Colored lithograph. SPM

84. Cameron gallery in Tsarskoe Selo. L. Premazzi. 1855. Water colors on paper. SLM

85. Travel in the coach. Unknown artist. The first part of the 19th century. Water colors on paper. SLM

86. Courier. König. The first part of the 19th century. Lithograph. SLM

87. Gate on the Moscow road. Gobert from the drawing of A.M. Gornostaev. The first part of the 19th century. Engraving. SLM

88. Russian village. J.A. Atkinson. 1803—1804. Engraving, aquatint, water colors. SHM

89. Lyuban bridge. From the original by G. de Tretter. 1823. Lithograph. SLM

90. Team of three horses carrying couriers. Gobert. 1838. Engraving. SPM

91. Summer landscape. K.F. Knappe. 1802. Gouache on paper. SHM

92. Village in winter. K.F. Knappe. 1797. Gouache on paper. SHM

93. Team of three horses. P.A. Aleksandrov. 1825. Colored lithograph. SPM

94. Coachman. H. Mitreiter. 1840s. Colored lithograph. SPM

95. Team of three horses crossing a river. P.A. Aleksandrov. 1825. Colored lithograph. SPM

96. Panorama of the bridge over the River Volkhov. K.P. Beggrow. 1825. Lithograph. SHM

97. Panorama of the Novgorod Kremlin. From the original drawing by A. Durand. 1839. Lithograph. SPM

98. The Sofia Cathedral in Novgorod. Unknown artist. 1830—1840s. Lithograph. SHM

99. Panorama of Novgorod. The copy of engraving by K. Nike after the drawing of Ch. de Lespinas. The end of the 18th—the beginning of the 19th century. Colored etching. SHM

100. View to the Novgorod Kremlin from the park. K. Burkovsky. 1862. Lithograph. SHM

101. Novgorod. View of the trade district from the park. K. Burkovsky. 1862. Lithograph. SHM

102. Sledge. B.-E. Swebach. 1830s. Lithograph, water colors, varnish. SPM

103. Russian escort. Unknown artist. The first third of the 19th century. Lithograph. SLM

104. Highway in winter. H. Mitreiter. 1830—1840s. Lithograph. SPM

105. Snowstorm. K.K. Schulz from the original by P.N. Gruzinsky. 1860s. Lithograph, colored print. SPM

106. The village church near Novgorod. Unknown artist. 1830—1840s. Lithograph. SHM

107. Bronnitsy. K. Williams from the original by R. Jonston. 1815. Aquatint, water colors. SHM

108. A peasant. C. Kohlmann. 1820s. Water colors on paper. SPM

109. Dance. A.G. Oubigan. 1821. Colored lithograph. SPM

110. Folk entertainment in Russia. K. Buddeus. 1820. Engraving, water colors. SPM

111. Russian post cabin. I. Stadler after the original by R. Porter. 1809. Engraving, water colors. SPM

112. Closed sleigh in a village street. P.A. Aleksandrov. 1825. Colored lithograph. SPM

113. Russian women. J. Laminith after the original by E.M. Korneev. 1812. Engraving, aquatint, colored printing. SPM

114. Valdai, district town in the Novgorod region. A. Voronetsky. The first third of the 19th century. Pencil on paper. SLM

115. Russian folk dance. K. Wagner after the original by E.M. Korneev. 1812. Engraving, aquatint, colored print. SPM

116. Vyshny Volochek. Unknown artist. 1802. Engraving. SPM

117. A peasant woman. K. Buddeus. 1820. Engraving, water colors. SPM

118. Vyshny Volochek. Vladimiro-Mariinsky Children's School of the Imperial Academy of Arts. M. Rashevsky from a drawing by Stepankovsky. 1894. Woodcut. SHM

119. A peasant house. K. Buddeus. 1820. Engraving, water colors. SPM

120. A boy, putting shoes woven of lime-tree bar on. Unknown artist from the original by K.A. Zelentsov. 1820s. Oil on canvas. SPM

121. Amusements of Russian maidens. From the original by Aubrun. 1822. Lithograph. SPM

122. Torzhok. Unknown artist. 1802. Engraving. SPM

123. View to Borisoglebsky monastery in Torzhok. Unknown artist. The middle of the 19th century. Engraving. SLM

124. The highway inn. From the original by Raffe. 1839. Lithograph. SPM

125. Sledge sliding. A.G. Oubigan. 1821. Colored lithograph. SPM

126. View of Tver. N.Ya. Sablin. 1769. Engraving. SLM

127. Tver. Otroch monastery. Unknown artist. 1830s. Water colors, gouache on paper. SPM

128. View of the city of Tver. M.F. Damam-Demartret. The beginning of the 19th century. Aquatinta, colored print. SHM

129. Tver. The administration building. Unknown artist. 1830s. Gouache, water colors on paper. SPM

130. Tver. Millionnaya Street. Unknown artist. 1830s. Gouache, water colors on paper. SPM

131. Klin. S. Poryvkin. 1859. Water colors on paper. SLM

132. Russian folk amusements. K. Wagner from the original by E.M. Korneev. 1812. Etching, aquatint, colored print. SPM

133. Swing. P.A. Aleksandrov. 1825. Lithograph colored with water colors and Indian ink. SPM

134. Coachmen. A. Orlovsky. 1820. Colored lithogtaph. SPM

135. Tverskaya tollhouse. F.I. Camporesi. 1789. Engraving, water colors. SPM

136. Petrovsky castle. E. Gostein from the original by V. Adam. After 1855. Lithograph, colored print. SPM

137. View of the State Orphanage and Kremlin from the Ustinsky Bridge. M.N. Vorobiov. 1818. Oil on canvas. SPM

138. Triumphal Arch by the Tverskaya tollhouse. Ph. Benois. After 1850. Lithograph, colored print. SPM

139. View of the Staraya Square. D. Lafond from the original by J. Délabart. 1801. Engraving, aquatint, water colors. SPM

140. View of the central Moscow. Au. Cadolle. 1825. Colored lithograph. SPM

141. View of the Kremlin near Kamenny Bridge. Unknown artist. 1790s. Engraving, water colors. SPM

142. View of the Kremlin from the Sofiiskaya Embankment. P.P. Vereshchagin. 1868. Oil on canvas. SHM

143. View of the Kremlin. F.I. Camporesi. The end of the 1790s. Engraving, Indian ink, water colors. SHM

144. View of the Iverskie Gate. A. Müller from the original by V.O. Vivien. After 1850. Lithograph, colored print. SPM

145. Teremnoy Palace in Kremlin. F.Ya. Alekseev. 1801. Oil on canvas. SPM

146. Bell-ringer. K. Buddeus. 1820. Engraving, water colors. SPM

147. View of the Ivan the Great bell tower. Unknown artist. 1825. Engraving, water colors. SPM

148. View of the Ivan the Great bell tower. L.J. Arnout from the original by D. Gagen. After 1850. Lithograph, colored print. SPM

149. View of the Boyarskaya Square in Kremlin, Teremnoy Palace and the Sacred Entrance Hall. F.Ya. Alekseev. 1800—1802. Water colors on paper. SHM

150. Trooping the Colors at Sobornaya Square in Kremlin. F.Ya. Alekseev. 1800s. Oil on canvas. SHM

151. View of Moscow Kremlin and Kamenny Bridge. F.Ya. Alekseev. 1810s. Oil on canvas. SPM

152. Inside view of Kremlin. I.F. Gärtner. 1838. Water colors on paper. SPM

153. The parade at the Red Square on the occasion of unveiling the monument to Minin and Pozharsky in February 1818. A. Afanasyev. Late 1810s. Engraving, water colors. SHM

154. The memorial to Minin and Pozharsky. Ph. Benois. After 1850. Colored lithograph. SPM

155. View to the Saint Basil's Cathedral. L.P.A. Bichebois from the original by V. Adam. After 1850. Colored lithograph. SPM

156. The Spassky Tower. J.-B. Arnout. After 1850. Colored lithograph. SPM

157. The Spassky Tower. A.F. Chernyshov. 1840s. Water colors, pencil on paper. SPM

158. View of Kamenny Bridge from Kremlin. A.V. Joli from the original by Au. Cadolle. 1825. Colored lithograph. SPM

159. The Pashkov Palace. L.P.A. Bichebois and M.Ch. Fichot after the original by A.Ch.B. Baillot. After 1850. Colored lithograph. SPM

160. Assembly Hall. A. Guedon, P.M. Roussel from the original by F. Dietz. 1840s. Colored lithograph. SPM

161. The Moscow courtyard. L. Korneev. 1840s. Water colors on paper. SPM

162. The New Stock Exchange and Gostiny Dvor. J.-B. Arnout from the original by F. Dietz. 1850s. Colored lithograph. SPM

163. View of Arbat Street. V. N. Nechaev. 1830—1840s. Water colors on paper. SPM

164. The Kuznetsky most. Au. Cadolle. 1825. Colored lithograph. SPM

165. Coachmen. A. Orlovsky. 1820. Colored lithograph. SPM

166. Peasant at a Moscow street. C. Kohlmann. Late 1830s. Whiting, water colors on paper. SPM

167. Russian folk games at the street. F. Dürrfeldt from the original by F.I. Gatterberger. 1790. Engraving, water colors. SPM

168. View of the Imperial Petrovsky Theater and its surroundings in Moscow. R. Kuryatnikov. 1825. Engraving, water colors. SPM

169. Teatralnaya Square. L.J. Jacottet, Ch. Bachelier from the original by Bronin. 1840s. Lithograph. SPM

170. Kuskovo. View of the usadba from the pond. N.I. Podklyuchnikov. 1836. Oil on canvas. SHM

171. Tverskoy Boulevard. Au. Cadolle. 1825. Colored lithograph. SPM

172. Rozhdestvensky Boulevard. S.M. Shukhvostov. 1840s. Oil on canvas. SPM

173. Tverskaya Street. Au. Cadolle. 1825. Colored lithograph. SPM

174. View of Tverskaya Street. F.Ya. Alekseev. 1810. Water colors on paper. SPM

175. White drawing room. V.P. Trofimov. 1900s. Water colors on paper. SHM

176. Study of the Grand Duke Sergei Aleksandrovich. A.P. Baryshnikov. 1902. Water colors on paper. SHM

177. View of the mansion of the Moscow Governor-General at Tverskaya Street. L.J. Arnout. 1840s. Colored lithograph. SPM

178. In a tavern. Unknown artist. 1830s. Colored lithograph. SPM

179. Coachmen in a tavern. A. Orlovsky. 1808. Colored lithograph. SPM

180. View of Lubyanskaya Square. L.P.A. Bichebois and P.M. Roussel after the original by F. Dietz. 1840s. Colored lithograph. SPM

181. Landau carriage. B.-E. Swebach. 1830s. Colored lithograph. SPM

182. Central post office. A. Müller after the original by F. Dietz. 1840s. Colored lithograph. SPM

183. Piligrims. Unknown artist. 1820s. Indian ink, water colors, pencil on paper. SPM

184. View to Novodevichy Convent. Ch. Bachelier after the original by I.P. Orlov. After 1850s. Colored lithograph. SPM

185. Panorama of Moscow from the Vorobyevy Hills. L. Deroy after the original by Au. Cadolle. 1825. Lithograph. SPM

186. View of Moscow in the time of Peter the Great. K.I. Rabus. 1846. Oil on canvas. SHM

187. Triumphal Arch at Myasnitsky Gate of Bely Gorod. P. Picart. 1710. Engraving. SHM

188. Coronation of Catherine I. Fireworks at Tsaritsyn Meadow on May 7, 1724. Unknown engraver. 1724. Engraving. SHM

189. Village of Izmailovo. Peter II going on a trip. I.F. Zubov. Later 1720s. Engraving. SHM

190. Coronation of the Empress Anna Ioannovna at the Uspensky Cathedral of the Moscow Kremlin. C.A. Wortmann from the original by O. Elliger. Engraving in the coronation book published in 1731. SHM

191. Fireworks display on April 30, 1730 during the festivities on the occasion of the coronation of the Empress Anna Ioannovna. O. Elliger from his own original. Engraving in the coronation book published in 1731. SHM

192. Ceremonial procession of the Empress Elizaveta Petrovna entering Moscow on February 27, 1742. I.A. Sokolov. Engraving from the coronation book published in 1744. SHM

193. View of Sobornaya Square of Moscow Kremlin during the coronation ceremony. I.A. Sokolov. Engraving from the coronation book published in 1744. SHM

194. Fireworks and illumination displays at the Yauza River near the Imperial Golovinsky Palace on June 3, 1742. J. Stenglin. Engraving from the coronation book published in 1744. SHM

195. Ceremonial reception of the Empress Elizaveta Petrovna at the Voskresensky Novo-Yerusalimsky monastery. M.F. Kazakov. 1790s. Engraving. SHM

196. Proclamation of the decree on the time of coronation of Catherine II at the Ivanovskaya Square of the Kremlin on September 18, 1762. A.Ya. Kolpashnikov from the original by J.L. de Vellie and M.I. Makhaev. 1827. Engraving. SHM

197. Ceremonial procession of Catherine II from the Kremlin Palace for the coronation at the Uspensky Cathedral on September 22, 1762. D.V. Andruzsky from the original by J.L. de Vellie and M.I. Makhaev. Engraving from the coronation book published in 1856. SHM

198. The intinction rite performed for Catherine II at the altar of the Uspensky Cathedral. T. Dmitriev from the original by J.L. de Vellie and M.I. Makhaev. Engraving from the coronation book published in 1856. SHM

199. Prechistensky Palace. Throne hall. Architectural drawing. M.F. Kazakov. 1774. Indian ink on paper. SHM

200. Petrovsky Travel Palace. F.I. Camporesi from his own original drawing. 1789. Engraving, water colors. SHM

201. View to Slobodskoy Palace and Dvortsovy Bridge across the river Yauza. F.I. Camporesi. Late 1790s. Engraving. SHM

202. Viphaniya or Spaso-Viphansky monastery. Workshop of F.Ya. Alekseev. 1800—1802. Indian ink, water colors on paper. SHM

203. View of the Triumphal Arch at the Strastnaya Square in Moscow. F.Ya. Alekseev. 1800s. Indian ink, water colors on paper. SHM

204. Troitse-Sergieva Lavra monastery. View of Uspensky Cathedral, bell tower and the Tsar's palace. Workshop of F.Ya. Alekseev. 1800—1802. Water colors on paper. SHM

205. Ceremonial founding of the Christ the Savior Cathedral on the Vorobyevy Hills on October 12, 1817. A. Afanasyev. Late 1810s. Engraving, water colors. SHM

206. Ceremonial procession of the Emperor Aleksandr I from the Kremlin Palace to the Uspensky Cathedral on August, 15, 1816. I.A. Lavrov. 1816. Water colors on paper. SHM

207. Proclamation of the decree on the time of coronation of the Emperor Nikolai I at the Red Square in Moscow. L. Courtin, V. Adam. Lithograph from the coronation book published in Paris in 1828. SHM

208. Procession of the Emperor Nikolai I from the Uspensky Cathedral after the coronation. L. Courtin, V. Adam. Lithograph from the coronation book published in Paris in 1828. SHM

209. The Aleksandrinsky Palace in Bolshaya Kaluzhskaya Street. Park façade. L. Picci. 1850s. Oil on cardboard. SHM

210. Visit to Moscow by the Emperor Nikolai I on October 28, 1837. P. Victor from his own original drawing. 1837. Colored lithograph. SHM

211. Ceremonial procession of the Emperor Aleksandr II entering into Moscow on August 17, 1856. L. Dumon after the drawing by M.A. Zicci. Woodcut from the coronation book published in Saint-Petersburg in 1856. SHM

212. Coronation of the Empress Maria Aleksandrovna in the Uspensky Cathedral. A. Siroy, Ch. Bachelier from a drawing by M. A. Zicci. Colored lithograph from the coronation book published in Saint-Petersburg in 1856. SHM

213. Formal dinner reception at the Faceted Chamber on the coronation day. E. David from a drawing by V.F. Timm. Colored lithograph from the coronation book published in Saint-Petersburg in 1856. SHM

214. Reception for the Cossack deputies at the Andreevsky Stateroom of the Kremlin Palace. A. Siroy, Ch. Bachelier from a drawing by V.F. Timm. Colored lithograph from the coronation book published in Saint-Petersburg in 1856. SHM

215. Illumination display and Emperor's procession leaving through the Voskresensky Gate of the Kremlin. G. Schwarz. 1856. Oil on canvas. SHM

216. Ceremonial procession of the Emperor Aleksandr II from the Uspensky Cathedral after the coronation. G. Schwarz. 1856. Oil on canvas. SHM

217. Illumination display at Ostankino during the coronation festivities. N.I. Podklyuchnikov. 1856. Oil on canvas. SHM

218. Ceremonial procession of the Emperor Aleksandr III from the Kremlin Palace to the Uspensky Cathedral for the coronation. V.V. Vereshchagin. 1883. Oil on panel. SHM

219. Imperial regalia. From a drawing by K.E. Makovsky. Colored lithograph from the coronation book published at Saint-Petersburg in 1883. SHM

220. Coronation of the Emperor Aleksandr III. From a drawing by I.N. Kramskoy. Colored lithograph from the coronation book published at Saint-Petersburg in 1883. SHM

221. View of the Kremlin from behind the Kamenny Bridge. From the series of paintings "Coronation illumination displays in Moscow. Coronation of the Emperor Aleksandr III". V.S. Rozanov. 1883. Oil on canvas. SHM

222. Illumination display in Moscow during the coronation of the Emperor Aleksandr III. View of the Christ the Savior Cathedral from a balcony of the Kremlin Palace. N.E. Makovsky. 1883. Oil on canvas. SHM

223. Gala performance at the Bolshoy Theater on May 18, 1883. From a drawing by S.F. Aleksandrovsky. Colored lithograph from the coronation book published in Saint-Petersburg in 1883. SHM

224. Ceremonial procession of the Emperor Nikolai II from the Kremlin Palace to the Uspensky Cathedral. N.S. Matveev. Early 1900s. Water colors on paper. SHM

225. Coronation ceremony at the Uspensky Cathedral. Nikolai II puts on the crown. From a drawing by E.P. Samokish-Sudkovskaya. From the coronation book published in Saint-Petersburg in 1899. SHM

226. Tverskaya Square. View from the mansion of the Moscow Governor-General. From the series of paintings "Coronation illumination displays in Moscow. Coronation of the Emperor Nikolai II". V.S. Rozanov. 1896. Oil on canvas. SHM

227. View of the Ivanovskaya Square in the Kremlin. From the series of paintings "Coronation illumination displays in Moscow. Coronation of the Emperor Nikolai II". V.S. Rozanov. 1896. Oil on canvas. SHM

228. Emperor Nikolai II and Empress Aleksandra receiving greetings in the courtyard of the Petrovsky Travel Palace. From a drawing by I.E. Repin. From the coronation book published in Saint-Petersburg in 1899. SHM

229. Emperor Nikolai II visiting the Troitse-Sergieva Lavra monastery on May 22, 1896. M.N. Belyaevsky. 1896. Oil on cardboard. SHM

Abbreviations:

SPM—State A. S. Pushkin Museum
SHM—State Historical Museum
SLM— State Literature Museum
RSL—Russian State Library

List of authors and sources of the quotations

Aksakov, Sergei (1791—1859),
    prominent public figure, author, journalist famous for the two volumes of his classic biographical writings published in 1856 and 1858.

Ancelot, François (1794—1856),
    well-known French poet. He came to Russia in 1826 as a secretary of the French ambassador. His book "Six months in Russia" published in Paris in April 1827 described the time of Nikolai I coronation.

Andreevsky, Sergei (1847—1918),
    poet, critic. The poem "Petropavlovskaya Fortress" was written in 1881.

Apukhtin, Aleksei (1840/41—1893),
    poet. His first collection of poems was published in 1886 in Saint-Petersburg.

Baratynsky, Evgeny (1800—1844),
    prominent poet. The quotation is from his poem "Gypsy maiden" (1830).

Batyushkov, Konstantin (1787—1855),
    prominent poet and author.

Bashutsky, Aleksandr (1803—1876),
    author, journalist, publisher, aide-de-camp of the Governor-General of Saint-Petersburg in 1826—1832.

Belinsky, Vissarion (1811—1848),
    famous liberal publicist.

Blagovo, Dmitry (1827—1897),
    published interesting reminiscences of his grandmother (1768—1861).

Bussier, Leon de,
    French nobleman who visited Russia and left reminiscences entitled "Travel in Russia in 1829".

Catherine II (1729—1796),
    the Russian Empress from 1762 to 1796.

Choiseul-Gouffier, Sophia,
: lady-in-waiting at the Russian Imperial Court from 1812. Her reminiscences of the period of 1812—1825 were published in 1862.

Custine, Astolphe de (1790—1857),
: French author who visited Russia and published a controversial book "Russia in 1839" in France. The book was prohibited in Russia for many years and first published in full only in the 20th century.

Dumas, Alexandre (1802—1870),
: famous French author who traveled over Russia in 1858 and published his travel diary in 1859.

Filimonov, Vladimir (1787—1858),
: poet who published the poem "Moscow" in 1845.

Gautier, Théophile (1811—1872),
: well-known French author who visited Moscow and Saint-Petersburg in 1858 and published a diary of his travels.

Gerakov, Gavriyl (1775—1838),
: author and historian who published in 1830 the diary of his travels in many regions of Russia in 1820—1821.

Gerstner, Franz (1793—1843),
: engineer who supervised the construction of the first railroad in Russia opened in 1837.

Glinka, Fedor (1786—1880),
: poet and publicist.

Glushkov published in 1802 a book of sightseeing information and advice for the travelers on the highway between Moscow and Saint-Petersburg.

Hagern, Friedrich (1794—1848),
: Dutch diplomat who traveled in Russia in 1839.

Knyazhnin, Vladimir (1883—1942),
: poet, author his poem "In Saint-Petersburg" was published in 1911.

Konstantin Romanov (1858—1915),
: Grand Duke, grand-son of the Emperor Nikolai I, poet, musician, President of the Russian Academy of Sciences. His diary was published in 1989.

Kukolnik, Nestor (1809—1868),
: poet, playwright, journalist.

Larreil, Jean Dominique (1766—1842),
: Napoleon's private physician, came to Russia with the invading French army in 1812. His diary yields interesting information about Russian life.

Lermontov, Mikhail (1814—1841),
: a great Russian poet. His "Panorama of Moscow" was written as a school essay in 1833/4.

Mey, Lev (1822—1862),
: poet, playwright. The quotation is from his poem "Smoke" published in 1861.

Miranda, Francisco (1750—1816),
: a South American public figure, traveled over 4 thousand kilometers throughout Russia in 1786—1787.

Mikhnevich, Vladimir (1841—1899),
: well-known journalist who compiled a guide book entitled "Saint-Petersburg at a glance" (1898).

"Moscow, Historical Guide",
: a four-volume guide book published in 1827.

Muravyev, Mikhail (1757—1807),
: poet, educator.

Nadson, Semen (1862—1887),
: poet, extremely popular in his time.

Nekrasov, Nikolai (1821—1877/78),
: famous liberal poet, journalist, and publisher.

Ogarev, Nikolai (1813—1877),
: poet, radical publicist in political emigration; his poem "Saint-Petersburg" was published in 1841.

Polezhaev, Aleksandr (1804—1838),
  poet.

Pushkin, Aleksandr (1799—1837),
  the greatest Russian poet and author.

Pylyaev, Mikhail (1842—1899),
  journalist who published several books on history and everyday life in Moscow and Saint-Petersburg.

Radishchev, Aleksandr (1749—1802),
  author and poet who was sentenced to death for his book "Journey from Saint-Petersburg to Moscow" that was judged to be "seditious" by Catherine II. Later the sentence was commuted to ten-year exile, the entire print run of the book was destroyed and only a few copies are extant.

Reinbeck, G.,
  German traveler who visited Russia in 1805.

Ricci, Louis (1800—1865),
  English author who visited Russia in 1835.

Schumann, Clara (1819—1896),
  German concert pianist who visited Russia in February—May of 1844 with her husband, the famous composer Robert Schumann (1810—1856).

Ségure, Louis Philippe de (1753—1830),
  French ambassador in Russia in 1785—1789 who traveled extensively throughout Russia.

Selivanov, Vasily (1813—1875),
  public figure who published his reminiscences in 1881.

Simborsky, Nikolai (1849—1881),
  radical poet, his poem "Statue" was published in 1877.

Sokolov, Pavel (1826—1905),
  artist.

Soloviev, Sergei (1885—1942),
  poet who later was ordained as a Russian Orthodox priest. His poem: "Saint-Petersburg" was in 1906.

Staël, Louise Germaine de (1766—1817),
  famous French author who visited Russia in 1812.

Stankevich, Nikolai (1813—1840),
  philosopher, poet.

Stuckenberg, Anton (1816—1887),
  railroad engineer and author who was involved in the construction of the Moscow-Saint-Petersburg railroad in 1842—1849.

Svinyin, Pavel (1788—1839),
  journalist, his book "Sightseeing in Saint-Petersburg and its environs" was published in 1816.

Tyutchev, Fedor (1803—1873),
  famous poet.

Ungern-Sternberg, Johann von,
  German traveler who visited Moscow in the summer of 1808 or 1809.

Vyazemsky, Petr (1792—1878),
  poet, òritic.

Weinberg, Petr (1831—1908),
  liberal poet, author.

Wilmot, Martha and Catherine,
  sisters from an English-Irish family who visited Russia in 1803—1807. Their diaries and letters to relatives describe their impressions of Russia.

Wistenhof, Petr (1811—1855),
  author who published "Essays on Moscow Life" in 1842.

Yakubovich, Petr (1860—1911),
  liberal poet.

Yazykov, Nikolai (1803— 1846/47),
  well-known poet.

Zhukovsky, Vasily (1783—1852),
  distinguished poet and courtier.

Contents

From Publishers
5

Introduction
6

Saint-Petersburg
13

"In carriage, in sledge or on foot..."
79

Moscow
131

Coronation festivities
179

List of illustrations
228

List of authors and sources of the quotations
236

Литературно-художественное издание

САНКТ-ПЕТЕРБУРГ — МОСКВА

Живописное путешествие из Северной столицы в Первопрестольную

Альбом на английском языке

Ответственный за издание
Г.М. Попов

Редакторы
Н.А. Федорова, Л.П. Ганичева, Т.М. Котельникова

Корректор
Е.В. Ваганова

Компьютерная верстка
А.В. Кочкин, Г.П. Ларин

Предпечатная подготовка
И.Г. Кабулов

Тираж 2500 экземпляров

Издательство «Интербук-бизнес». Лицензия № 02643 от 28.02.2000
Россия, 123104 Москва, Спиридоньевский пер., д. 12/9, офис 11
Телефон: (095) 200-64-62, факс: (095) 956-37-52
E-mail: info@interbook-art.ru
О книжных новинках издательства можно узнать на сайте: www.interbook-art.ru